Jasper Bennett

Pedagogical ideals

As Portrayed by Leading, Living Educators

Jasper Bennett

Pedagogical Ideals
As Portrayed by Leading, Living Educators

ISBN/EAN: 9783337280673

Printed in Europe, USA, Canada, Australia, Japan

Cover: Foto ©Paul-Georg Meister /pixelio.de

More available books at **www.hansebooks.com**

PEDAGOGICAL IDEALS

AS PORTRAYED BY

LEADING, LIVING EDUCATORS.

BEING A COMPILATION OF THE BEST THOUGHTS OF
MANY OF THE LEADING EDUCATORS OF THE
DAY UPON LIVING EDUCATIONAL ISSUES
AND ACTUAL SCHOOL-ROOM LIFE.

BY JASPER BENNETT.

CHICAGO:
A. FLANAGAN, PUBLISHER.
1888.

PREFACE.

The excuse offered by the author for presenting such a book as this to the public is a desire to save to the teaching profession the many gems or crystallized thoughts, relating to the teacher and his labors—but which, valuable as they appear—otherwise must have been lost.

These thoughts emanated from the minds of leading educators of the present day and have nearly all been uttered or written during the past four years; and while some matter presented may not appear to come up to the "ideal," yet, in the main, it approximates the ideal sufficiently to justify the title of the book.

Much that is written upon the various interesting topics of the times in which we live reaches us through the columns of popular magazines and periodicals of the day, is read with or without comment, is then, in most cases, carelessly cast aside, and in a few short months almost wholly relegated to oblivion.

Even though the theme be of momentous import, the author of world-wide fame, and the language of classic merit, its common fate is that of one of our meanest daily newspapers.

The author, while reading the leading educational journals of the United States during the past four years, has been enabled to collect and preserve the material for this little volume—collected and arranged at first for his own reference and pleasure. But he has concluded, at last, that the collection merits publication and that other teachers should share the riches of this little store.

This necessitates a very considerable second culling, and though the elimination brings it down to the present limits, yet there may be some superfluous matter left. However, it is well to remember that the book as a whole represents the thoughts of many persons, and that any apparent superfluity is but a preservation of individuality.

Again, it may contain some apparent or real contradictions upon a given theme. But it should be considered " all the more " a broad-gauge view.

'Tis hoped that some of the great army of teachers will find in it something to commend, something that will inspire them to higher aims and greater effort; and that if there be a faltering one who is down-cast and discouraged, he will read and catch the inspiration, resolve, and *re-resolve*.

In the preparation of this work the author acknowledges his indebtedness to the *New York School Journal*, *New England Journal of Education*, *American Teacher*, *Tennessee Journal of Education*, *Intelligence*, *Education*, and other professional journals; and for the original thought give credit to the following leading educators, most of whom are Americans and most of whom are living:

A. D. Mayo.	Joseph Payne.	Jas. A. Garfield.
R. W. Boyd.	Joseph Lukens.	Charity Snow.
G. E. Gorden.	Prof. Huxley.	J. H. Seelye.
A. R. Sabin.	G. Stanly Hall.	E. E. White.
S. H. Lockett.	O. B. Bruce.	Pres. Noah Porter.
Aaron Gove.	David W. Hoyt.	A. E. Winship.
Julia A. Pickard.	W. H Payne.	B. F. Patterson.
Prof. John Ogden.	Adolf Deisterweg.	E. F. Mead.
Anna C. Brackett.	Hiram Orcutt.	John W. Dickinson.
T. W. Bicknell.	Ida A. Ahlborn.	M. A. Newell.
Ex-Supt. Doty.	Gen. John Eaton.	Miss M. V. Gillin.
Supt. Edgerly.	Rev. Mr. Frisbie.	M. Jules Ferry.
Prof. J. T. Hand.	Dr. Tingley.	J. L. Pickard.
Prof. Sacket.	Dr. J. H. Kellogg.	George H. Cook.
C: E. Meleney.	Jacob Barhite.	Wm. M. Giffin.
N. E. Leach.	W. N. Barringer.	Wm. F. Fox.
G. W. Hoenshel.	W. H. Venable.	George D. Shultz.
Eva M. Tappan.	E. D. Brinkerhoff.	Edward Brooks.
Miss Bancroft.	S. P. Robbins.	J. S. Babcock.
E. M. Harriman.	Solomon Sias.	Amanda J. Young.
Lillian M. Munger.	Prof. Raab.	Marion Talbot.
H. S. Jones.	Williard Brown.	J. W. Dowd.
Geo. A. Littlefield.	H. S. Tarbell.	Col. F. W. Parker.
	Miss Wadleigh.	

Martinsville, Ill.,
Dec. 24, 1887.

J. B.

CONTENTS.

CHAPTER I.

CHAPTER II.

CHAPTER III.

CHAPTER IV.

CHAPTER V.

CHAPTER VI.

8 *Contents.*

CHAPTER XI.

CHAPTER XII.

PEDAGOGICAL IDEALS.

PUBLIC SCHOOLS. AND WHAT IS EXPECTED OF THEM.

CHAPTER I.

SKILLED INDUSTRY.

In an article written by the Rev. A. D. Mayo, a few years ago, the following expressive language was used: The best friend of every youth should now tell that youth, that character and trained power are the only assurance of success in this country. Every church in America should be warned, betimes, that without intelligence and practical holiness no sect of religionists will be found worthy to greet the Lord when He comes in His new Kingdom. The aspiring young politician should get on the school committee, study the resources of his state, and preach the gospel of *skilled industry* from the *"furrow up to the Senate"* or *he will not carry the election twenty years hence,* at the crisis of his career. The American girl, however gifted or highly born, who can not fashion a home with her own brain, will always be a dependent upon society and a hanger-on in the social paradise that is to be. In this law there is no exception of race, or class, or profession, section, party, or creed. If the people of Louisiana, down in its cypress swamps, put more brains into their heads for the next half-century than the people of New England, the Creole will go up and the Yankee go down. The gospel of educated labor, the expert in every profession, the man fitly trained

always in the right place, is the one impartial message of
the hour to all men, women, and children on American soil.
Many there will be who will not heed it; and they will go
the way of all second-rate people in all ages and lands.
But they who hear and do, will be saved, and lead the Republic along the line drawn by the finger of Providence
toward the America that is to come.

THE NEW EDUCATION.

That same writer, two years later, said of "The New
Education" and its aims: It is first a revival of faith in
human nature itself, as that nature reveals itself in childhood.   Instead of imposing a theory on the child to mold
and fashion him into a given shape on the one hand, or
concentrating all his powers on the work of making himself a practical success in life on the other, it proposes to
develop the child into the most complete manhood or
womanhood possible for his order of ability and natural
endowment.   It believes in child nature, and studies it
with the hope of finding out the beautiful, divine ways by
which the child shall become the woman or man.   And it
believes that the child, thus trained for character and such
ability as belongs to it, will in the end be a far more valuable member of society than if molded into the imitation
of any other man, or fashioned to a machine for any special
work.

Further on he says of "The New Education," It holds
that the thing taught is of less importance than the spirit
and the method in which everything is taught; the object
being not to cram the mind with knowledge, but to im-
plant the love of truth, and to train the faculties to find it
by vital contact with nature, humanity, literature and life.
In character-training the New Education accepts without
question, the Christian method of love, in the noblest

Christian meaning of that mighty word. It believes that labor can be raised above drudgery into a region of joy and hope, and does not despair at once, of obtaining accurate knowledge and dutiful conduct, and making the life of a child joyous and beautiful, with the beauty of courage, faith, and boundless hope, and trust in God."

IGNORANCE OF VOTERS.

In his first and only inaugural, the lamented Garfield gave utterance to the following: But the danger which arises from ignorance in the voter cannot be denied. It covers a field far wider than that of negro suffrage and the present condition of that race. It is a danger that lurks and hides in the courses and fountains of power in every State. We have no standard to measure the disaster that may be brought upon us by ignorance and vice in citizens, when joined to corruption and fraud in suffrage. The voters of the Union who make and unmake constitutions, and upon whose will hangs the destiny of our government, can transmit their supreme authority to no successor save the coming generation of voters, who are sole heirs of our sovereign power. If that generation comes to its inheritance blinded by ignorance and corrupted by vice, the fall of the Republic will be certain and remediless. The census has already sounded the alarm in appalling figures, which mark how dangerously high the tide of illiteracy has risen among our voters and their children."

UNIVERSAL EDUCATION.

In an address before the State Teachers' Association of South Carolina, in 1886, the Hon. R. W. Boyd made use of the following language: It is for universal education, if it can, to change the temper of the people, re-awaken the patriotic spirit, recall the old pride in the Republic, inspire

to the loving and intelligent discharge of civic duties, and
make the people feel that with all draw-backs they have a
great country, and the best government under the sun.
.   .   .   .   Let education undertake and accomplish its highest work; let universal
education, furnished with bountiful hand by the State,
supply proper training for citizenship, and then with virtuous and intelligent mothers, with a press in the hands of
culture and patriotism, and with churches full of zeal and
good works, we might hope to see the old pride and faith
return. We could hope to see political life and methods
purified and elevated, honesty and capacity fill the public
offices, and each new political question easily and happily
met and answered.

FREE EDUCATION.

The Rev. G. E. Gordon, of Milwaukee, Wis., a few
years ago, while criticizing Richard Grant White's paper
published in the *North American Review*, December, 1881,
expressed the following opinion of the American idea as to
purpose of free education.   .   .   .   .   "The
uncultivated masses of Americans simply think of the
public schools as means of giving their children a chance
to get a better living. Cultivated people, whether poor or
rich, think of the schools as at least providing a certain
mental furniture for children's minds, whereby they may
make use of the advantages which a free social competition
offers them. Thoughtful people believe that whatever
amount of education can raise a person in the social scale,
tends to make that person respect both his own opinion
and that of others. But neither class of people would be
foolish enough to believe that book-learning and thrift, or
book-learning and good citizenship are so directly connected as to be always found together. Mr. White's state-

ment that the only justification for sustaining the public schools at the public expense is that, but for them, life, liberty, and property would be unsafe, *is very weak.* The most that is advanced under this head, in favor of schools, is the general truth that they make *life more worth living* by increasing its horizon, *and liberty more enchanting* by enlarging its possibilities, *and property more desirable* by developing the advantages of its possession. Knowledge introduces us into a world full of chances *which are denied to the illiterate.* . . . . However we may lament a defective method in education, or lament the defective material upon which it has to act, *the thing itself* is, beyond question, one of the most potent agencies in the advancement of modern society. Education supplies its possessor with efficient help to satisfy physical wants. Education *sees* wants, in the person of its happy possessor, which lead him to rise into a more virtuous position in society. And in both ways men are removed from the temptation to ordinary crimes, and society saved from corruption. Education is the mightiest machine we have for the civilization of the world. Americans already believe this, and are not asking shall the people be educated? But, How best can we reach all classes with our schools, especially the lowest and poorest? And as we answer this question with a practical mind we shall best satisfy the demands of the age.

EDUCATION IN LANGUAGE.

At a public meeting of educators, but recently, PRES. J. H. SEELYE, of Amherst College, advanced the following thoughts:

The education which we need is, largely, an education in language. Language is not only the form of thought, but it represents the very body of thought itself. All possible achievement of thought, therefore, in science, nor art, nor study, can possibly furnish so copious a discipline of thought, a discipline so rich, so varied, so comprehensive, so complete, as language itself. The child's development of thought will be found to proceed, step by step, with his development of language; and as in every vital process, so here, the product of life is also the reproducer and strengthener of life. A very large proportion of time and effort spent in education should be given to language. —*Almost the largest proportion,—certainly it is not easy to make this too large* The only way in which the child can be taught to know the real mind of the people among which he is born, is by the study of their language, and the only way in which he can grow up to be a living and influential member of the nation or race of which he is to form a part, is, by first becoming facile in the language wherein alone the true life and inner spirit of the nation or race is expressed. The true heart of a people is uttered only in its speech, and the only way in which we can get access to the heart, to move and mold it, is by its speech. Teach the child language, then. *Teach him his mother tongue.* Give more room for writing, reading, and spelling in our schools. We need not disparage scientific and practical education; but this comes later, and belongs properly to the grade of the professional school. *Common schools are not professional schools,* and we shall make a great mistake if we start the professional training too soon."

WHAT OUGHT TO BE EXPECTED OF OUR SCHOOLS.

Prof. A. R. Sabin, Principal of Franklin School, Chicago, in stating what he thinks "Ought to be expected of the public schools," begins with a quotation from the constitution of Illinois: The General Assembly shall provide a thorough and efficient system of free schools, whereby all the children of the State may receive a good common school education.

He then continues : If these State Constitutions be further inquired of it will be found that nearly all of them set forth in a Bill of Rights that religion, morality, and knowledge are the necessary conditions for permanently securing to society the inalienable rights of life, liberty and the pursuit of happiness.

To meet these three necessary conditions we recognize three agencies—the church, the home, and the school. The church and the home have their existence in society, and are not called into existence by the State; their existence antedates that of the State. Their function, therefore, is not prescribed by the State. What is the function of each?

It is the function of the church to teach religion.

It is the function of the home to provide for, to care for, and to secure the physical, moral, and intellectual well-being of every child born into it. The mission of the church is a divine one, ordained of God. So the Christian church holds, and so I believe.

It is the function of the school to impart knowledge. Called into being by the State, the schools can claim no diviner origin than that of human wisdom, fore-sight, and prudence. From their origin and function they may be properly termed secular. Such they are and such they ought to be.

Human *foresight* has seen that without the free schools not all the children of the State will have the means of obtaining a good common school education.

Human *prudence* has established the school for the training of children in useful knowledge.

Distinct as are these three agencies, the church, the

home, and the school in their origin and function, they are
closely interwoven in our Christian civilization. They are
all a part of it, are necessary to it, and have one common
interest, viz.: the realization of the greatest good of all.)

It is deemed important to this discussion that the relation of the school and the home be determined, to the end
that the question of religion and morals be impartially
considered, and certain responsibilities rightly placed.
Many persons have claimed that religion should be taught
in the schools. It is here claimed that the responsibility
for direct religious teaching rests with the home and the
church, but that both the church and the home have a
right to demand that all such religious teaching be treated
with respectful and sincere reverence by the schools. In
reverence for things held sacred and divine the school
should be the intelligent and sympathetic ally of the church.

While the relation of the school to the home is a very
close one, yet the school is not the home, nor does the
teacher stand in *loco parentis* to the child even while at
school. Protection the school affords. It may be more
moral than the home; the teacher may be a kinder and
more helpful friend than the home affords; yet the school
does not clothe nor feed the child,—does not minister to
it in sickness,—does not bury the dead,—keeps no vacant
seats.

In morals the school ought to aim at nothing less than
what the best home realizes. The pure should be kept
pure. The vicious should be shown the better way. And,
yet the school is not responsible for failures in the matter
of morals. · The school does not see the child during the
first five years of its life. The home has had the twig-
bending all to itself during these first years.

The schools deserve credit for undoing a world of mischief, but they do not merit censure for failing to undo it all. . . . . The home is responsible and can not delegate its responsibility; nor does a good home wish to do so. As a patron of the public schools I desire that in matters of personal, vital religion, my child be let alone; that in the realm of morals, the instruction be so conducted that the right and the true be made always to sit on the right hand, the wrong and the false, on the left.

More than one respectable writer is charging failure upon the public schools because of alleged immoralities among school children. A boy swears. Is it more likely that he acquired the habit at school, where he is under control and supervision, than at home, on the street, or in the saloon? . . . . A boy tells lies. Let the decrier of the public schools acquaint himself with that boy's nursery before fixing the responsibility elsewhere. A boy is leprous with all that is unclean, impure and vicious. Will any honest man dare affirm that such a boy has a pure home or one that has followed his going out and his coming in?

While Mr. SABIN did not state definitely ALL that is expected of the public schools, his statement of the case is so replete with "good things" that the author finds ample excuse for giving it a place in this chapter.

WHAT SHALL BE TAUGHT IN OUR SCHOOLS.

But, following it under the head "What shall be taught in our common schools" an article written for the *"Tennessee Journal of Education"* in 1883 by PROF. S. H. LOCKETT, of Tenn., the line of demarkation is much more definitely drawn as to what should be admitted into the common school curriculum. Omitting some preliminaries, the thread runs thus:

My present purpose, however, is to answer the question 'What should be taught in our American schools to the great masses of youths and children of both sexes, who attend them; who have neither time nor means for mere culture; who, on the contrary, can scarcely afford to acquire the rudimentary equipment for the stern battle of life, into which they are drawn before the period of adolescence is passed?' Some parts of the answer to this question are so patent, that it needs nothing but the bare statement of them to command the assent of every one.

Reading, spelling, writing, and arithmetic, all will acknowledge as indispensable branches of study, no matter what sphere of life is to be occupied. But there is another important question to be answered concerning these fundamental and essential branches. How much of each of these should be taught to every child, and how much time should be devoted to them? In replying to these inquiries, I doubt if I shall do so to the satisfaction of any person but myself, but I hope to be able to give some good reasons for the faith that is in me.

Every child should commence to read as soon as it enters school, and its reading lessons should be continued uninterruptedly until it can read intelligently any ordinary composition in its own language. Whether it can read in accordance with the elaborate rules of the treatises on elocution or not, is a matter of utter insignificance. If it can read silently, without moving the lips, so as to understand thoroughly the meaning of the printed or written matter before its eyes, that is the main point. For that is the kind of reading most of us are called upon to do in our actual lives. Perhaps one in ten thousand may be called upon, occasionally, to read aloud; but it most generally happens that even that one *is self-called,* and *is a great bore to the rest of the ten thousand.*

How reading should be taught is not my purpose to discuss; nor, in fact, the methods of teaching any of the branches of study, except incidentally in this article.

Spelling, like reading, should be taught, during the child's entire school life, as it is of great importance, and unfortunately to an English speaking person, the most difficult of all things to learn well. But every person ought to learn how to write the ordinary colloquial and epistolary language of his native speech with fair correctness. Whether any one can stand head in a "spelling bee" or not is unimportant. *Oral spelling is of no value, either as training or an accomplishment.*

Writing should be taught during all of the school years, so that every child by practice shall acquire a plain, legible hand-writing, which it can execute with facility and without fatigue.

.   .   Every child should learn arithmetic, of course; but when, how, and how much of it? These last are vital questions, and an unwise neglect of a due consideration of them has done more harm to the school-life of untold millions of children than could be by any possibility overestimated.

A child should begin to learn arithmetic the very first day it enters school, no matter how young it is. It should be first taught to count correctly, if it has not already acquired that knowledge at home.   .   .   From counting it should be led by easy steps to the writing and reading of numbers, and then to the performance of simple calculations in the four fundamental rules; always without being wearied and overtasked. And through the first three or four years of school-life arithmetic should be taught gradually, easily, and pleasantly; and in this brief period *all the arithmetic likely to be needed in after years can be acquired.*

Yes, I honestly believe that a child of average intelligence can be taught *between the ages of seven and twelve years,* all the arithmetic it will be called upon to use in any ordinary life. I know that from ten to twelve years is generally devoted to arithmetic in our common schools, but I consider it a fearful loss of precious time. A loss because so many other useful things could be learned in those years, when the mind is young and receptive—a loss of time because a great deal of the arithmetic learned is never applied in after life. I have no hesitancy in asserting that in all the city of Nashville, with its busy inhabitants, including men in all the trades, occupations, and professions, there can not be found one-half dozen men, who have been called in real business transactions to use one-half of the rules and operations given in the ordinary school arithmetic. Yet children are made to plod and worry through these useless rules with utter disregard of the time expended.

The addition, subtraction, multiplication, and division of simple numbers, of denominate numbers, of common and decimal fractions; the old rule of three or simple proportion; involution and evolution; the simplest cases of percentage and interest embrace about the amount of arithmetic needed in business life. My own life has necessarily made me deal largely in mathematical problems, but except in my capacity as a teacher, I never had to use more arithmetic than above enumerated.   .   .   In all my life I have never known of a really difficult problem to arise in actual business transactions, and yet the arithmetics used in our schools are filled with involved and ambiguous examples which puzzle even experienced teachers to unravel. Away with such utterly useless, beclouding, and obscuring of the otherwise beautiful and simple science of quantity! . . . But, if arithmetic is to be made so easy, some will ask, "from whence are you to get your mental training?" I answer. "By going ahead into new fields of intellectual development."

. . Let algebra and geometry take the place hitherto occupied by arithmetic during the last three or four years of school life (of many children). Both of these branches of mathematics are more easily mastered, than the latter part of most text-books on practical arithmetic, as many teachers will testify. And both of them are more useful in common life. . . . . Algebra is a far more powerful and easily managed means of analysis than arithmetic, so that problems which are difficult to state in arithmetical language are readily rendered into an algebraic expression, and the solution follows as a matter of course. Every teacher is aware that he never troubles himself to solve a complex problem by arithmetic, but at once applies his algebra to it and robs it of all its difficulty. Why should not the same means be given to every child in our schools? Beyond a doubt, every child can and ought to be taught so much algebra as to enable it to use the literal notation and signs and symbols with facility, and to state problems in the form of equations. So much algebra would do away with half the rules of arithmetic, by substituting in their stead formulas; would rob all the inverse problems of percentage and interest of their terrors, by bringing them under one set of simple equations in which the only possible variation would be a mere change in the required quantity; would relegate to the limbs of obsolete and useless lore compound proportion and arithmetical analysis; would illumine with a flood of light which would sweep out of existence all that conglomeration of ill-stated, badly-constructed puzzles called Miscellaneous Examples.

As to the propriety of introducing geometry into our common schools, even of the lowest grade, if taught in a commonsense, practical way, there can be no possible doubt. Not one man or women, no matter how high or low be the station occupied, but needs in daily life a correct knowledge of magnitude and form. That correct knowledge can come only from a study of geometry. Such knowledge will aid the farmer in laying out and measuring his lands and buildings, the merchant in planing his residence and store-house, the carpenter and bricklayer, the stone-cutter and quarryman, the tinner and blacksmith, the founder and machinist, the dirt-digger and rock-breaker. It will help the ladies in their ornamental work, in the decoration of churches, and, in fact, in ways and places innumerable. This knowledge can easily be acquired by all, and at the same time a very useful training be gained in drawing and designing.

.　.　Geography and history, which are generally considered as among the most essential of school studies, I have purposely left out of the curriculum, till here.

That geography should be taught to very young pupils I freely concede, for it can be made interesting to them, and is an excellent means of awakening observation and attention. Coupled with map-drawing, geography can be made useful in other directions, which it is needless to more than merely indicate. But that any child in the world should be forced to go through in succession the child's first, the primary, the second, the intermediate, the high-school, the higher, and advanced geographies, I shall never voluntarily give my consent. In the first place each of these graded geographies repeats its predecessor almost slavishly, simply using bigger words in the definitions and descriptive portions as the advance is made. Second, the child sickens and becomes disgusted with the same dreary repetition of barren names and unimportant facts, as it completes book after book, and finally gets to hate the very name of geography before the long list is half finished. Third, the knowledge gained from the study of geography is, most of it, utterly valueless, and insignificant, and a great deal of it is not true, when taught. Of what possible importance is it to any human being, except, perhaps a Maine lumberman, that the Androscoggin river rises in Lake Moosetocmaguntic, and flows south and then east and then south again into the Casco Bay? Or who cares to know that the town of Wattawamkeag is situated at the confluence of the Penobscot and Wattawamkeag rivers, and has so many inhabitants?

Besides the uselessness of such knowledge, it is the most fleeting and difficult of retention of all knowledge. No human mind can or ought to retain such trash, and so far as my experience goes, the average mind simply refuses to do so.

I have in my life made an actual survey of one State, and made a map of it. It took me five years to gather the data and make the map. I visited every town, village, cross-road, ferry, etc., in the State, located them on the surface of the earth, and on the map, yet, I can not to-day, remember the names and localities of a hundredth part of them, nor do I wish to do so, if I could. But, some one will say, you need geographical knowledge when you travel. *No, you do not.* Go to the nearest ticket office, say where you wish to go, and the agent will sell you the right ticket, and a map with the route marked out upon it in a big black or red line, so broad you can see it across the room. *If you depend upon your geographical knowledge as a guide in traveling, you can not go ten miles from your home*

without being inextricably lost. So let us abolish at least
one-half of the geographies—it matters but little from
which end of the list we cut off the discarded ones.

As for history, I would say use some good history
always as a reader, suitable to the stage of advancement
of the pupil, and by means of it try to teach the child to
read understandingly. But for poor humanity's sake do
not compel children to learn history "oy heart."

Grammar should be taught to every child, every day
during its school life; by the teacher's example of correct
speech, and the correction of every error of its own speech.
Theoretical or philosophical grammar should undoubtedly
be kept for the last days of school life, as it can be profit-
ably studied by advanced pupils only.

Now after this elimination of the branches usually
occupying the attention of the school, the question naturally arises, what can be substituted in the place of those
left out or cut short. I answer, the elementary natural
sciences; physics, chemistry, physical geography, botany,
physiology, and astronomy, with some music and drawing.
I know many will sneer at this long list of 'ologies and
deny their utility, and the practicability of teaching them
in the common schools. . . . . What
can be of more importance to any human being than a
knowledge of the laws of nature as manifested in the
world of animate and inanimate objects with which he
comes in daily contact by the aid of his senses? Should
not the air we breathe, the water we drink, the food we
eat, the earth we cultivate, the flowers that bloom around
us, the rocks which make our mountains and with which
we build our houses, the animals we domesticate, the stars,
and sun, and moon, which hang overhead, and the bodies
within which our immortal souls reside possess some inter-

est to us? And should not each human being have at least an elementary knowledge of the laws which regulate and govern all this grand cosmos of which he, to himself at least, is a most important part? To these questions there can be an affirmative answer, only. And every one can have a really useful knowledge of nature, if proper means are taken to teach that knowledge, and the golden hours of youth are utilized as they should be, instead of being wasted, as is so often the case·

It is but justice to Prof. Lockett, that it be said, he believes in a classical education, so far as higher education is concerned, and if one could afford time and means he would say, 'The classical is a solid and safe foundation upon which to build one's own self-development, in any department of intellectual activity.'

In the March, 1886, number of *Education*, the Rev. A. E. Winship says. . . . . It is clearly an educational blunder to train our school system to æsthetic perfection, and then, by a law of compulsory attendance, confine children in schools that are as ill adapted to their needs as a hot-bed is to an oak. The public school must be specifically adapted to the greatest possible good of those who most need its influence. Wisdom, expert skill, fervent spirit, must be utilized in devising and applying systems and methods of giving the greatest possible benefit to those who will instinctively *drop out of school ranks before they are half through the grammar school course.* If the most needy three-fourths of the children of our cities and manufacturing towns are never promoted throuhg the grammar school, it is a fatal error to magnify the promotion idea until it sends the non-promoted out into life with little other remembrance of school-life, than that it was a perpetual failure with them. . . . . If

America is to Americanize the multitudes from all lands
and climes; if she is to have a home-loving, patriotic, loyal
people, developed from the heterogeneous mass of humanity within our borders; if she is to have rectitude, integ-
rity, and virtue developed in the boys and girls born of
vicious parents, bred in poverty, schooled in crime; if she
is to have her wealthy citizens enjoy the grandeur of American scenery better than the classic ruins of Greece and
Rome; if she is to have her æsthetic sons love the home
comforts and rustic graces of America better than the
fashion and frivolty of Paris; if she is to have her literary
aspirant appreciate Bryant, Lowell, Longfellow, Whittier,
Irving, Hawthorn, and Emerson as well as the British
verses of legendary days; if she is to have her newspapers
loyal to American progress rather than British greed, she
must adopt the public school to the demands of the day.
There must be reform. *In place of the patch-work reading-
book* with a square of prose and a square of poetry set with
matronly exactness there must be reading enough to form
character and direct reading habit. In the place of the
classics of antiquity and fables of England's mythological
days *there should be American classics* with the sufferings and
heroism, the character and glory, the consecration and
devotion of the Puritan, the pioneer, the frontiersman, and
the revolutionary saint.   .   .   .   .   In schools
for the poor and for the peculiar foreign elements massed
in large cities, *let there be less technicality, less unreasonable
drill in precision,* a winnowing of the subjects to be taught,
an adaptation of the school to the individual, temporal, and
moral necessities and loyal requirements of home, society,
and nation.

COURSES OF STUDY.

In a small and unpretentious journal styled the *Normal Teacher,* published at Covington, Indiana, in

February, 1887, the following was found, over the single
letter C : Courses of Study.—Everywhere the people are
discussing the courses of study. Much progress has been
made within the last twenty years, and much greater will
be made within the next ten years. The schools should
prepare children for the world, and not for college. The
school should touch the world as it is. The question
asked everywhere is:—What should our sons and daughters learn in order to prepare for any station in life? College and school boards have been slow in their progress,
but some day these tardy boards will wake up and find
that a progressive board has been selected for the purpose
of sweeping the sham course of study out of the schools.

Teachers say to pupils: Now, if you will take the
High School course, pass all your examinations, and go
through the routine of school regulations, you will be prepared to enter the Freshman course in the university.
Even some school men have gone so far as to tell pupils
that the completion of the courses of study in the High
Schools will admit them to the Sophomore class. Here
they add a falsehood to their enthusiasm, which in after
years pupils will find out. We want more true honesty
and less flattery. We need more thinking and investigating, and less standings and grades. Many pupils spend
more time studying how to PASS, than in investigating the
subjects pursued.

Three-fourths of the graduates of the city schools are
no better prepared for the fierce battle of life when they
get through the High School than when they entered it.
The strong essentials of an education have been neglected.
They have uttered a few scientific terms and learned the
names of a few things, *but the uses of none.* They can name
a few literary men, but they have never tasted the kernel
of literature.

Many things that are in our course of study should be omitted or given a second place.

Every student should possess the power to think logically and quickly, to speak easily and fluently, and to write correctly and rapidly.

In the public schools *all pupils* should learn to read well; . . . be able to write a good letter; know the history of the country sufficiently to become intelligent citizens; know a fair amount of the geography of the United States; understand the laws of health; be taught to hate tobacco and alcohol; learn the story of the wonderful march of the human race across the centuries; learn so much arithmetic as is necessary for the duties of business life; be able to write plainly and with ease; have inculcated honesty, truthfulness, punctuality, industry, and a respect for the rights of others. Good manners should not be neglected.

Pupils are pushed too rapidly in the higher studies. Many pupils who are hurried through to graduation, learn in after years that they have been greatly injured. The so-called higher branches can be quickly learned, if the foundation is good. . . . Let us strive to give our pupils a good practical education, and to develop all that is good and valuable in human nature. Pay less attention to graduation, and more to developing manhood and womanhood.

APPLICATION OF KNOWLEDGE.

In the *New York School Journal* of Jan. 29, 1887, the following editorial comment was noted: It is an acknowledged principle that knowledge is not power unless applied; in fact, learning and knowledge may become burdensome weights, text-books may be memorized with no profit, and the possession of facts may become a hindrance to success.

Unless the possessor of knowledge can apply it in some way in life, it would have been better for him not to have had it. The minds of children may be crammed full of all sorts of material, but all this load will be a positive hindrance to success until it is in some way applied. We want knowledge that can be used to-day. The needs of the world are urgent—never more so. Our schools must waste no time in making pupils learn what they will, in all probability, never use. Cut down arithmetics, grammars, histories, by this standard. Let the most rigid severity be used. The idea that *our public schools must give a general culture is exploded,* and that other idea that the *mind must be filled with knowledge against a possible time of need,* that probably will never come, is exploded also. We have often asked 'what will be the fate of a girl upon the streets of a great city like New York, knowing Latin but not sewing; able to tell a hundred dates in history, but ignorant of bread-making; able to demonstrate the binomial theorem, but not able to keep a set of books; competent to find the value of x in a quadratic equation, but not knowing the value of money; accurate in drawing a diagram of Africa, but utterly unable to draw a working diagram of her own dress? Knowledge that does not touch the work of life is well nigh useless, for the work of life is just now urgent, and men and women are in great demand who can do that work.   .   .   .

REFORMS IN EDUCATION.

On the same page of the same Journal in issue of Feb. 5th, 1887, the editor applies the "utilitarian theory" to "higher education" in commenting upon the courses of study in colleges and high-schools.

He says: Reforms in education work their way from above down. If a boy is designed for college, his course is early shaped by what colleges demand as admission, and what kind of learning will help his standing when he enters one. Quite an amount of Latin, Greek, and mathematics, a little English grammar, no English literature of any consequence, a little of either German or French, will admit him to *any college in our country.* These requirements *make* the courses of study in our most advanced normal schools, because it is *their* design to prepare their graduates for principals of high schools, fitting students for college. Would it not serve the cause of thorough education just as well to make Greek optional in a college course, to be commenced after a student has entered, if at all? Would it not also be just as well to relax the requirements in Latin, and much increase them in science, English literature, and composition? Can not just as much study be gotten out of chemistry, botany, physics, and English, as from Latin? We are living in an age preeminently distinguished for its scientific and mechanical inventions. At no time during the history of the world have there been so many books published, and so many papers printed. We need chemists, botanists, zoologists, geologists, mechanical engineers, builders, writers, and off-hand public speakers. We want men conversant with modern literature and able to write fluently and correctly in at least two languages. We must have men and women of good common sense concerning the things of to-day, able to discuss with reason the issues which this new era has forced upon us. Work and thought have altogether changed since fifty years ago. In these new times new men are needed, filled with modern ideas, abreast with the age, and well established in morals. *Our colleges must supply this material.* They must not only *not* relax their thoroughness but must increase it, not by means of knowledge of the culture of the past, but through the solving of the hard problems of the present. It is a good omen that many old institutions are waking up to a realization of the *necessities* of the case.

FUNCTIONS OF THE AMERICAN SCHOOLS.

The judgment of Prof. W. H. Payne, of Ann Arbor, Michigan, will go far toward settling almost any contro· versy pertaining to things of an educational character. Here is an extract from a paper prepared by him. It bore the title 'Functions of the American Public School,' and was read at the meeting of the National Educational Association, held at Topeka, Kas., in 1886. Prof. Payne says: As the primal right of the State is that of self-preservation, the education that it may enjoin upon all is that without which good citizenship is impossible. The essential elements of good citizenship are intellectual pene-tration and breadth sufficient to distinguish between right and wrong, the just and the unjust, truth and error; the knowledge needed for individual guidance as a man, a citizen, a parent and a bread-winner; obedience to civil and moral law; physical soundness, patriotism, industry, economy. All these qualities are implicated in instruction and discipline.

It is not to be presumed that the school is to be held responsible for *all* that is essential to good citizenship. The co-operating influences of public opinion, the family, the church, the press, the court, etc., are assumed, and the State puts upon the school the duty of supplementing or complementing the work of these other agencies. As intel-ligence, discipline, and knowledge are the foundation and condition of all the civil virtues, the distinctive function of the public school lies in three lines.

Probity, accuracy, and industry are school virtues, the

almost necessary results of its organization, instruction, and discipline; and when the pupil becomes a citizen these become cardinal, civic virtues. The minimum of instruction that will answer the needs of the State and that should be obligatory, may be stated as follows: Skill in reading sufficient to interpret ordinary written composition; writing that is facile and legible, and the ability to speak and write the vernacular with facility and accuracy; some knowledge of American literature, and arithmetic sufficient for all ordinary computations; comprehensive knowledge of general geography, and a minute knowledge of home geography; a good knowledge of American history, and of our governmental machinery; a comprehensive knowledge of general history, and of the sciences, chemistry and physics; a knowledge of those parts of physiology that discover the art of healthy living; and a knowledge of the principles of morality, of economy and of Republican government.

There are breakers ahead, no doubt, and though free education may not suffer wreck, yet she should be piloted clear of all suspicious appearing matter floating upon the great ocean of universal knowledge. As to some of the dark appearing objects of which she should steer clear, an unknown writer gives some hints in the following:

OVERLOADING OF THE SCHOOLS.

There is a tendency on the part of the friends of the schools to over-load them, and impair their efficiency, by assigning to them, in addition to their own proper work, the work of the family, the church, the Sunday school, the shop, and various benevolent institutions.

Are the children of from four to six years of age in the way at home; try to smuggle them into the already over-crowded public schools and thus convert said schools into day nurseries.

Is there any philanthropic or benevolent enterprise in contemplation; the public schools are thought to be the most inviting field for operations.

Is religion thought to be a desirable thing: the schools are called upon to teach it, and the teacher who wisely thinks it best to hold his school to its own proper work and not to dissipate his pupils' energies upon a number of outside matters runs the risk of having his school denounced as Godless and himself as an infidel.

Is temperance thought to be a good thing, immediately the school-master is called upon to teach all the minute effects of alcohol upon the system, even to its effects upon the molecular structure of the various tissues.

It is found by experience that through culpable neglect of mothers, many of their daughters are not taught to sew, cook, and perform the various household duties in a proper manner, it is insisted that sewing, cutting and fitting, cooking, and the multifarious duties which our girls may be called upon to perform, must be taught in the public schools.

Is it observed that a majority of boys in towns and cities must follow some mechanical pursuit, it is urged that the trades, or, at least, some of them should be taught in the schools,—that is, we must have industrial training, and the boys must be initiated into all the mysteries of toe-nailing, blind-nailing, and nailing flush; of chamfers, modeling, embossing, etc.

INDUSTRIAL SCHOOLS.

The tendency is to introduce everything into the schools regardless of time, expense, or consequences.

The Hon. John W. Dickson, of Massachusetts, has said, but recently, ... One defect charged against the work of the school is the failure to train children in independant use of the mind.   To remedy this, *the orderly use of tools is recommended.*   Yet mere manual dexterity is the result of imitation, and great manual skill is found in persons of little culture.

It appears that ample provision for general intelligence should be provided before special training, since the *intelligent man is more important to the State than is the skilled artisan.*   The fundamental idea of education is the *superiority of man* to his '*uses.*'   This, the language of experience and philosophy teaches and directs to *other* than "*industrial methods*" for its accomplishment.   If children can not do independent work at graduation, it is because they were not allowed to work independently in the class-room.   One may use a book and be ignorant of its truths.   The *abstract use of words* cultives the *passive powers only.*   All this is changed when *things* take the place of words.   The pupil becomes an investigator and will find an investigation within himself.   .   .   .   The object of the public school is to develop the child and bring him to his special work with *trained powers.*   Then let the technical and *industrial* schools prepare the way for active life.   .   .

The same writer, still later, has said: There is a growing sentiment in favor of directing public instruction towards that general development of the individual which will make a *man* of him, and fit him to enter with intelligence upon any work to which his capacites, and his inclination may finally lead him.   The proper function of the public school is to furnish the occasion of symmetrical human development.   Human development is produced by the *right exercise* of *power.*

With the last few hints at the probability of 'Industrial Training' being laid upon the already overloaded educational wagon, the author leaves the subject to be discussed by the living educators and statesmen of the day. It is fast becoming one of the issues of the times in which we live.

Industrial Schools are in demand and are on the increase. The only question is, "Can the State undertake to give Industrial Training to the masses?" If not, then, to only a portion of her citizens(?) To what portion? And who posesses the divine right? Can the State discriminate in this matter? If so, in favor of whom? Can the citizens of a state, by their ballots, legalize, and their posterity tolerate discriminating legislation upon this vital subject? Or shall the whole matter be forever relegated to private institutions? The experiment was born there and is being tested. Meanwhile thousands of bright-eyed boys and girls are growing on to maturity without the benefits,—getting knowledge in the abstracts, whilst the practical side of nature in them lies dormant and undeveloped. The author knows that this is "utilitarian doctrine." But, be it known, he is on that side of the issue. He believes it to be within the possibility of any State in the Union, to put this matter to test, and that, too, by impartial legislation, and that no great stretch of time need elapse ere it comes to a trial.

CHAPTER II.

THE TEACHER, CHARACTER, ATTAINMENTS, CULTURE, DUTIES, AND RESPONSIBILITIES.

FITNESS FOR TEACHING.

"Fitness for Teaching," as understood by Payne in his "Outlines," involves two factors—"Natural aptness and acquired ability." "Under the last term is to be included the results of experience. *Poeta nascitur non fit* is a general formula, Poeta standing for lawyer, merchant, physician, carpenter, teacher or farmer. Freely translated it means this: 'Eminent success in any department of labor is conditioned on an innate prediliction for it.'

Natural aptness for teaching is especially indicated by two qualities,—the love of knowledge and governing ability. He who is fond of knowledge and is conscious of possessing it, naturally desires to impart it to others. A school must be brought under the teacher's control before it can be successfully instructed. Discipline is natural and easy for some, while for others it is difficult or impossible, because it is unnatural.

No one can become a good teacher who is not a good student. One chief purpose of instruction is to create and foster a zeal for study; but the teacher cannot impart a warmth that he does not feel.

The teacher's knowledge should comprehend much more than the subject matter of his daily lessons; and constant acquisitions should be a law of his life.

The good disciplinarian is one born to rule,— one to whom is given a marked degree of co-ordinating and executive ability. The mind cannot be instructed unless it be in a fit attitude or posture; but children, especially in masses, will not voluntarily assume and keep the proper attitude.

Order, promptness, a respect for the proprieties of life, are among the best fruits of good instruction. They are invaluable both as an end and as a means.

Natural ability in the teacher, however great, should be supplemented by professional study

Society may as properly require a preparatory training of the teacher as of the lawyer, the physician or the divine; it has as clear a right in the first case as in the others, to protect itself from empiricism. Professional teachers should be men of science; their power of precision should enable them to construct wisely and well; and the power of revision to reconstruct on a rational basis. This reconstructive ability should determine three things : existing defects, their cause, and cure.   .   .   .   .   .

Progressive self-improvement in method is the duty of every teacher. The means of self-improvement are the following: The study of one's own practice with a view to its amendment; observing the methods of other teachers; the study of Educational Science through educational literature.

Continuing in the same line of thought is an extract from the pen of JOSEPH F. LUKENS:

THE TEACHER'S CULTURE.

Every profession requires a general and a special preparation. A general knowledge of the common branches will not make a teacher. A special professional education is needed in addition to the general culture. Lack of preparation is the great fault in those who essay to be teachers. There are more failures from low grade scholarship than from any other cause. The teacher must have a thorough

and fresh knowledge of what he teaches. He should have
such a knowledge that he would be able to teach if the text
books were burned. Teachers of to-day need all the culture and training they can acquire. The topics can never
be so thoroughly mastered but that something new may be
learned. In each new class will be found some new phase
of character,— some mental peculiarity never before presented.

The teacher who sits down in the belief that he has
learned all that can be learned of the topics assigned to
him, or the wants of his grade, will soon find his task less
pleasant and his success less marked.

It is the teacher's duty to notice little things,—to
become attentive to small formalities. Discipline is made
up of these minute formalities. When the teacher has
learned how to repress his inclination to scold or punish
and has acquired the habit of noting the manner of performing the smallest formalities, he is on the road to
success.

No teacher is strong enough to force a whole school at
once. A wise teacher will conquer chaos and caprice by
introducing order in little things. The teacher who is
strong enough to secure the performance of *one* of these
small formalities can secure *everything* by persistence.

. . . To the youthful teacher: Think more
and do more for the health of your pupils. Do you see
that girl yonder with a puffed unhealthy looking face?
What is the matter with her? See how tightly she is
laced; she can scarcely breathe. Perhaps that is the matter with her. At all events she is losing her vitality, and
will enter womanhood a mere wreck unless something is
done to relieve her, soon. It is within the province of her
teacher to look after her health. What can you do for her
and for others in like condition?

Think and do more for the *hearts* of your pupils. There is such a thing as heart culture; in fact, if there were not, man would be a monster. Study more than ever before how to cultivate the *souls*. Do you know what to do to make a soul grow? By sermons(?) That is a great mistake. Be sure that no day passes that you do not by a settled plan contribute to the growth of the hearts of your pupils.

Think and do more for the *minds* of your pupils. It is possible that you were in a groove during your last school, and that with the best of intentions you stayed there. The study of arithmetic, grammar, and geography is not enough;—these work but partially. You want to reach the whole mind. Boundless possibilities!

THE ETIQUETTE OF TEACHING.

"The Etiquette of Teaching" from an unknown writer, is to the point, and must occupy this place.

In and out of school, the teacher should avoid the company of persons who refuse him the respect due to his station, and should train himself to be able to do without them. The plea of having no one else with whom to associate is worthy very little, even if urged in strict accordance with truth. If you observe this rule, you shall rise; if you violate it, you shall fall.

Be careful how you do anything unusual before children. They will speak of it in other places, and without intending harm, give an imperfect or distorted account of the transaction, leaving out some salient point, or that which is the most important incident of all, perhaps.

If it be worth your while to make a rule, it is worth your while to observe it. If you make many rules, one will interfere with the other. It may sometimes happen that you yourself will forget one of them, and that the children noticing the fact will remind you of it. This, you must admit, would be very disagreeable. There are many little things done in school, of no harm in themselves, but inconsistent with perfect order. If you forbid these, you are bound to take care that they do not occur again, or, if any of them be repeated, to punish, in some way, the disobedience. You will find it, almost without exception, the case that they take place at the time some matter of real and pressing importance claims your attention, and when, of course you are not at liberty to deal with them. Before making a rule against a petty thing, consider whether or not the good resulting from its discontinuance will repay you for the time lost, the labor expended, and the severity required in enforcing the rule, and also whether the act is likely to fall into disuse as general good order advances.

Do not allow yourself to fall into the habit of giving, unasked, a reason or an explanation for everything you do or require to be done. Do not train pupils to expect it. It is not necessary, and you would find it very inconvenient at times. Besides, there are many persons to whom explanations sound very much like excuses. This does not apply to the subjects you teach, or to occasions when new plans are to be introduced or important changes effected.

It is a great advantage to bear in mind fully and clearly the occurrences of yesterday and former days. To be able to recall every particular, as occasions require, proves solicitude for the welfare of your pupils, and strengthens your influence with them. They have so little of importance to think about, except 'school' that they can not understand how the teacher could forget anything connected with it.

An imprudent teacher stretches his authority to persons and things that are not under his control, thus provoking and encountering opposition. Some persons yield to him; but while yielding revile him. Others resist, and he, being powerless to enforce obedience, is discomfited. Discomfiture of this kind,—of any kind, in fact,—lessens a teacher's influence. All teachers may have read that "To govern others you must govern yourself." It is a truth of which teachers should never lose sight, for in their case this self-governing means, not controling the temper only, but in everything else, keeping within bounds of the duties of their office. So long as one confines himself within the sphere of his labors it forms his proper protection, but as soon as he goes beyond it he exposes himself to injury and offense.

Again to young and subordinate teachers,—Center in yourself the authority of your school; the possession of it makes you more useful to your pupils and less troublesome to your superiors. You cannot have an orderly school while you favor the boy who is above his fellows in height or age,—while you connive at or suffer to pass unpunished in him sayings or doings that you would not permit in another. Such a one is more likely than any of the rest to take liberties, and it happens in many cases — from indolence or want of confidence on the teacher's part—that his assumptions meet but feeble resistance. The teacher's duty, in all such cases, is to act with a moderate share of resolution, and if he neglects to do this, he must be prepared to pay the penalty of his unworthy conduct.

Children sometimes appear to suppose that, so long as they are submissive to their teacher, they may be as rude and insolent as they choose to other persons; no teacher should foster such an opinion or even tolerate it for a moment. And though zeal for the school or the teacher himself may cause pupils to manifest violence in speech or action,—yet the teacher should promptly condemn such conduct. He has the right to demand that pupils deport themselves as gentlemen and ladies even when not in his presence.

It is unwise to display partiality for children who are favored by nature, or by fortune, in good looks, or in the easy circumstances of their parents. If favor be shown to any, those who, from obvious causes, may expect but a small share from others have the best claim upon the teacher. Bear in mind, 'he who favors is unfit to rule.' Every child in the school no matter what are his dispositions, habits or circumstances, is entitled to the full measure of fair play. Of course this fair play does not forbid the teacher to recognize and commend deserving pupils. But, if a teacher, without regard to merit, singles out one of his pupils as his companion and uses him as a spy, or a person to be spoken to when speaking of the rest, he reveals a weakness and shows that he is but imperfectly qualified to govern children. It is unfair to set any child upon his school-fellows as a spy. The person so employed, if continued in office any length of time, will finally, after the manner of all favorites, presume too much upon his patron and give offense. Then sooner or later he must be degraded and punished, and from that time he will look on the teacher with dislike, justly regarding him as the author of his disgrace. If a teacher desires to govern his pupils with ease and credit to himself he must not favor any of them. So long as his measures have no other object than the securing of what is agreeable to himself, and conducive to his own ease, so long will he be at strife with his school.

And last, but not least,—the annoyance teachers suffer from pupils and others out of school.

To pass it over without comment could serve no good purpose. The better course is to examine the evil calmly, and enquire how it may be remedied, and to what extent. When assailed by persons who have never attended his school, it ought to give him very little concern, since he is in no way accountable for their misconduct. But if those who offend him are, or have been under his care, he should, at once perceive and acknowledge that the cause of the grievance is his own faulty management; and further, that while he pursues an arbitary and unreasonable line of conduct in school, where, in a great measure, the children are in his power, he must expect that—upon obtaining the mastery, which they really do after leaving school—meeting him in public, they will repay his injustice with interest."

MODEL SCHOOL.

An eminent speaker, in addressing a body of teachers at Detroit, but recently, said: Have a clear, well-defined idea of the kind of school you want. Have in mind an imaginary model-school, but do not be discouraged if you fail many times before you attain this; for each day's determined work, will bring it nearer. Teach pupils how to study. Teach them how to get from a book the thoughts which it contains.

Much time is wasted in getting ready for work. Too often when a visitor enters the room there is the appearance of getting ready for inspection.

Teach pupils to attend to the business in hand, to do the work assigned them at the proper time, and to do *one thing* at a time.

In having recitations, be interested yourself, be enthusiastic, and have a soul in the work.

If you are obliged to punish, do it out of school,—or not in the presence of other pupils.

If anything unpleasant has occurred during the day between teacher and pupils, never allow the school to close without dropping some pleasant word, which will cause all to leave the room with a good feeling.

Cultivate in pupils, as far as possible, self-respect and self-government, and never attempt to ferret out mischief without certainty of success.   Better let it pass than fail in the attempt.

It is not necessary, in governing your school, to lower yourself to the level of your pupils; but always be dignified in your deportment in all the little things pertaining to government of your school, thus silently and imperceptibly lifting your pupils up to a higher standard.

CHARACTERISTICS OF THE TEACHER.

The following is a translation from the French *L'enseignement Primaire:*   The teacher should be modest in his tastes and manners as well as in his language.   In speaking to his pupils he should be careful to make use of only simple expressions which they can easily understand without effort.   He should, therefore, lay aside all affectation, and everything which flavors of pretension or pedantry; otherwise he will run the risk of laboring in vain.   He may utter torrents of eloquence, learned words, choice expressions, without exciting the least smile of intelligence, —the sign which shows that he is understood; while if he adapts himself to the children's understanding, he will see their faces glow with pleasure and joy, as they learn of things interesting to them and of which they were before ignorant.

The teacher should be active, of engaging manners, and should have a great amount of energy.   Nothing is to be more regretted than a kind of slowness or dullness characterizes some teachers. It seems as if they had to exert themselves extraordinarily to make the slightest movement. Consequently the school suffers and languishes, and if any progress is made it is only moderate.

We know that children have a tendency to imitate and copy all they see and hear, and to assimilate the qualities of a teacher, even his faults. So it is not astonishing if those who attend such a school as we have mentioned, become stupid, idle, careless, and good for nothing.

What a contrast with the class whose teacher is full of zeal, energy and activity! All the scholars are constantly occupied. He puts so much life and feeling and soul into the lessons as to hold his scholars, so to speak, fast to his lips, they are so afraid of losing one of his words. While teaching one class his watchful eye overlooks the entire school; he follows the doings of the other groups, entrusted to his assistants or to his monitors, in the smallest details. In this way his efforts are crowned with complete success, and the enthusiasm and ardor with which he is animated are communicated to his scholars, and leave profound and lasting traces.

HINTS FOR THE SCHOOL ROOM.

Still another anonymous article is here submitted. It was clipped from the Pennsylvania *School Journal* and contains the following thoughts:

Earnest, conscientious, progressive work, is the central idea of school management. The underlying principles of school instruction is to elevate the scholar to a higher plane of thinking, acting and being. To this, all discipline tends; in this all methods converge. The end is not to be obscured by irrelevant issues, or merged in the machinery of order and the adjustments of an elaborate system. We must have, first of all, honest work with reference to the mental and moral requirements of the pupils; and no amount of display, in the school-room or on exhibition days can atone for the lack of earnest labor as the chief essential of school life. Rose water is not a beverage, nor is confectionery strong meat or healthful food.

But in work as in everything else, there is a right way and a wrong way. A burden may be carried to a destined point by being dragged over the ground under the lash of the task-master, or, *it may be borne on willing shoulders*, with songs of praise and a shout of *"harvest home."*

Certain requisites of a school-room make it pleasant and lighten the labors of its inmates. There must be plenty of fresh air, comfortable seats, and a proper admission of light, without exposure to draughts. More than all, there must be scholars anxious to learn, and teachers able to impart instruction. There must be enthusiasm on the part of the Master, and a generous response of affection and interest on the part of the scholars. There must be a living principle, growing stronger and stronger, day by day, *that knowledge is good and desirable, that virtue is both right doing and right thinking*, and *that duty*, great or small, is the *true end and purpose of life*

Good order is essential to a well-regulated school-room; without its harmonizing influences all progress would be lost in the general chaos. But order is not the chief end of school-life. In some schoolrooms there is too much order. The inmates seem to be under a spell of enchantment. In such schools the quiet is so oppressive and awe-inspiring that the children are afraid to speak above the low tones which are usual in houses of mourning or among the tombs. There is no tyranny or cruel discipline here,

not even the sight of a rod,—only the low, dreary, monotonous voices of the teacher and children engaged in the
cold, hard, mechanical routine of question and answer.
The order is excessive,—overwhelming. It permeates
every part of the room. A laugh in such a school would
be altogether out of place. To drop a book or pencil
would be a catastrophe.

THE SUCCESSFUL TEACHER.

The following appeared in *The New York School Journal*
Oct. 6th, 1883. It is presumed to be an editoral.

Of many occupations it is said that there is no royal
road to success. How is it with the teacher? It certainly
would be a difficult matter to give a set of ready-made
rules by which a teacher of only average ability and in
ordinary surroundings may push ahead; but still, there are
a few essential considerations to which every teacher
should attend, and, doing so, may reasonably look for a
fair degree of success and promotion.

There is a two-fold work to be done in teaching as in
other arts; a two-fold success to be achieved, artistic success and business success. Each has distinct methods,
and both are honorable. But with the true teacher, as
with the true artist, artistic success is first sought. First,
to *be* a success, then to *make* a success; to *be* a GOOD TEACHER,
then to *be known* as one. To attain both of these ends, the
teacher must be a reader, a listener, a thinker; above *all* a
worker. By energy and activity he must compel the attention of parents. He should not, after a merely formal in-
vitation to parents to visit his school, allow interest to die
out. Parents ought not to be suffered to lapse into indifference concerning their children. They must be impor-
tuned to investigate, and make suggestions regarding the
teacher's work. He need not sacrifice his dignity in the

position. He will rather enhance it by trying to create public spirit in the matter;—to invite discussion through every possible channel,—in the school-room, in the parlor, in public meetings, through the churches, on the street, in the local paper,—everywhere. He should claim a certain monopoly of time and attention, not for himself, but for his work; and as a true teacher, he can not fail to believe in the justice of this claim.

The real importance of teaching, its heavy responsibilities, its grand and almost infinite possibilities,—all these must be deeply felt by the teacher; and through his efforts, felt by the parents and the community. By this means, individual teachers will help themselves, and the cause of teaching everywhere will be elevated to its true position.

HINTS TO YOUNG TEACHERS.

Containing some excellent thoughts, *Hints to Young Teachers*, is from the pen of CHARITY SNOW. One of the difficult things for the young teacher to do is to draw the line between an egotistical independence,—a feeling that "I don't care what people say," and undue sensitiveness about their opinions. Perhaps more overstep the line on the latter side than on the former. You are young, hopeful and enthusiastic. Your every plan seems to you so very desirable—that you have gotten, perhaps, just a little bit ahead of every body else. You look to see your scholars seize and act upon your new plans with avidity, and the parents and overseers of the school applaud. In short, you expect to make quite a revolution and win renown.

But nothing of the sort happens. Everything goes on both in school and out, about the same old way. Some criticise behind your back, of which you are sure to hear, some advise you not to try too many new notions, and some are very indifferent, to say the least. So you come to feel that your teaching is a failure, and that it is no use for you to try. You are chagrined, grieved, and humiliated, and the interests of the school suffer sensibly from your depression.

This trial may come through various causes,—methods of teaching or of discipline, or too little or too much of the social element, and your mental thermometer rises and falls as public opinion is for or against you. Now, while you must have a due regard for public sentiment, it must not be your conscience. You cannot change your measures according to this or that criticism, — cannot cater to the whims of all yours critics.

If you be successful you must cultivate a sensible, steady, mental habit, not too easily elated or depressed, — learning all you can from observation and experience, and holding steadily on your way with a degree of assurance, which, while it should not border on egotism, should keep you in a state of equanimity. Perhaps this can be attained only by long practice, but you must come to possess it, either by nature or by acquisition. Do your best always. If people seem friendly, believe them and take the comfort of it. If they seem unfriendly and cold, don't believe them. Keep your mental temperature so warm and equable that you shall disarm prejudice by the power of your own ingenious manners.

When you find things going amiss and yourself the subject of remark, a most excellent way is to look the matter over, and have a candid and calm talk with the disaffected ones. In nine cases out of ten fault-finders will modify their opinions. Perhaps you will yours somewhat, and thus, serious trouble will be averted. A pupil will often carry home a one-sided story of some punishment, and the parents may feel aggrieved, very much. If you can make it convenient to talk the matter over soon, with them, without excitement, you will usually find that they will approve instead of condemning. One instance on that special point is here given.

A lady teacher had occasion to punish a boy some ten or twelve years old. The punishment was two or three strokes of the ruler on the hand, then to be left standing on the floor near a warm fire. In a few moments, upon looking at the boy, she saw that he was faint. She sent him into the open air and he soon returned all right. His father was a very sensitive man where his children were concerned, and very much inclined to pick flaws with teachers. She was wise enough not to wait for the story to spread through the district,—the story, "That the teacher punished Georgie C. by feruling and then made him stand on the floor till he fainted away." But when school was out, she went straight to the business place of the father, and told him the exact circumstances.

She said to him, "I know it has a bad look, but I have told you the exact truth, and you can question any of my large, reliable scholars about it if you wish. I am sorry it happened so. I intended no undue severity. I choose to tell you myself before you hear exaggerated reports."

Perfectly pleasant, he replied "That is all right Miss ————. I am glad you came to me. If Georgie needs punishing, of course you are at liberty to do it. He faints very easily,—always did from a little child. A slight hurt or fright always makes him faint." He then bowed her out with as much sauvity as though she had greatly honored him by chastening his boy. And when gossips ran in to talk the shocking affair over, he knew all about it, and the excitement soon died out. This was a striking instance of "getting the inside track."

The teacher upon rehearsing *the* story to a friend, said, "If you think it was easy for me to go to him, you are very much mistaken. But I have saved myself a precious row."

But teachers cannot pass through such experiences repeatedly, and come out of them successfully. Such instances must not often occur, if one would stand secure. Such an experience safely passed is a good lesson for any young teacher. For a young teacher is only a scholar in the great school of life,—still undisciplined, in need of some sharp and wholesome lessons, and the only way to acquire the lessons of experience is to do the work. Others can not do it for him.

ELEMENTARY TEACHING.

Of elementary teaching PROF. HUXLEY said, also, There are a great many people who imagine that elementary teaching might be properly carried out by teachers provided with only elementary knowledge. Let me assure you that that is the profoundest mistake in the world. There is nothing so difficult to do as to write a good elementary book; and there is nobody so hard to teach properly and well as people who know nothing about a subject; and I will tell you why. If I address an audience who are occupied in the same line of work as myself, I can assume that they know a vast deal, and that they can find out the blunders that I make. If they do not, it is their fault and not mine; but when I appear before a body of people who know nothing about the matter, who take for gospel whatever I say, surely it becomes needful that I consider all that I say; make sure that it will bear examination, and that I do not impose upon the credulity of those who have faith in me.

In the second place, it involves that difficult process of knowing *all you do know* so well, that you can talk about it as you con talk about your ordinary business. A man can always talk about his own business. He can always make it plain; but if his knowledge is mere hearsay, he is afraid to go beyond what he has recollected, and put it before those who are ignorant in such a shape that they shall comprehend it. That is why, to be a good elementary teacher, to teach the elements of any subject, requires most careful consideration if you would be master of the subject; and if you are not master of it, you have need of familiarizing yourself with so much as you are called upon to teach—soak yourself in it, so to speak— until you know it as part of your daily life and daily knowledge, *and then you will be able to teach anybody.*

That is what I mean by practical teachers, and although the deficiency is being remedied to a large extent, it is one that has long existed. And it has existed from no fault of those who undertook to teach, but until the last score of years it absolutely was not possible for any one, in a great many branches of science, to get instruction which would enable him to be a good teacher of elementary things. . .

VISIT THE HOMES OF THE PUPILS.

An unknown writer regards it as a teacher's duty to visit the homes of his pupils. He writes as follows: The teacher who would be successful must win the confidence of his scholars and be in sympathy with them; he must know their natures, their surroundings, and their needs. In no way can he better do so than by visiting their homes. He shows his interest in them and wins their love, thereby. How such visits enable you to bind the children's hearts to your own! I go round in the district and see the parents, brothers and sisters of my pupils. I am shown a favorite picture-book, a pet dog, or pussy, or pony, or a little garden, over which a pupil exercises absolute ownership, and afterward I take occasion to inquire about these things.

I ask one whether his big brother has gone into that big store to clerk yet; I tell another that I never saw such a saucy little dog as hers; I recall some pleasant incident of my visit to their house; or ask Johnnie whether he can manage the potato bugs in his garden yet. In this way I gain the love, confidence, and hearty co-operation of my scholars.

The parents, too, are pleased with the attention, and no longer regard me as merely a school teacher, but more as a friend. My experience proves this an excellent way of securing the support and co-operation of parents.

Besides, I get many valuable hints. I learn that the most effective way to manage Willie R., if he does amiss, is to drop a line to his mother. I know that Jennie B. is to have a certain beautiful apple-tree as her own if she maintains her standing in her class, and that suggests a way of getting her to study. I find out what course of discipline the several families endorse, and that shows me what mode of punishment will be most judicious and effective with different pupils, in case I must resort to punishment. I learn, too, the likes and dislikes of the district, and those of the children, and that saves me from making mistakes in seating schoolars, enables me to avoid unpleasantness of various kinds.

These calls are beneficial to myself. I find men who can teach me many things about the practical affairs of life. I find that in some things I have much to learn yet, myself. I get more correct views of life, expand, and get upon a higher plane.

INDIVIDUAL INSTRUCTION.

Another writer says: The most efficient teacher is she who acquires the skill to reach the entire class as though they were one, making each pupil feel as if he were receiving the full measure of her instruction.

Forgetting this, many teachers miss their golden opportunity by being too individual in their instruction, thus losing forty pupils, and leaving them free for mischief while dealing with one. Giving special attention to one may be needful at times, but the occasion is rare. Reach the one through the many, is the highest principle to be adopted in the school-room. The results of such a course are not to be seen in a day, but will, ultimately, pay the price.

"BE YE KIND TO ONE ANOTHER"

was the text a teacher placed upon the blackboard, from which to speak from time to time to her pupils, enforcing the truth it contained by many an illustrative story and incident, until she had created a public sentiment in her school, making it uncomfortable for a pupil, through anger, jealousy, or envy, to be unkind to a playmate and worse yet to the teacher.

If one-tenth of the words some teachers use in scolding, fretting and fuming about the disobedience of pupils were used in creating a public sentiment in favor of charity and kindly forbearance, the average school would run itself without disciplinary friction.

There is in any school a liability to the development of a clique or ring, who succeed, if not counteracted, in making a sentiment which pays a premium upon illegitimate fun,—such as rough jobs, coarse jokes, applying opprobrious nick-names and playing mean tricks upon schoolfellows, and in ways innumerable revealing a tantalizing disposition or a tormenting spirit. It is a wise use of time for any teacher to use extra efforts to thwart the machinations of unscrupulous pupils who attempt to be leaders of such cliques,—thwart them by creating a counter public sentiment.

TEACHER'S TEMPER.

This little gem is from the German. The teacher should avoid a display of anger or bad temper. There are days when nothing seems right. All is wrong. If one inquires whether he has made any mistake, he will usually find the fault to be his own. He was not, perhaps, sufficiently prepared, or was disturbed by some incident at home; but he should never grow angry. Many a person has made himself unhappy for a life-time by some rash, thoughtless deed. Never be the *slave*, but the *master*, of your temper. Be very careful never to inflict punishment when laboring under excitement.

KNOWLEDGE BY HARD EFFORTS.

From the *American Teacher :* Knowledge is best that comes by hard effort, and it is best because of the effort, and not because of the knowledge. Effort that has a high motive in connection with it is best, and *it* is best not because of the *effort*, but because of the *motive*. Knowledge is not much if it be the end and the all.

The teacher is not the giver of knowledge. He is not the full reservoir from which the pupils are to draw supplies of fact and theory at will. He is the awakener and quickener of the knowledge-getting faculties of his pupils. He is the artesian well-driver, connecting the power of the pupil with the resources of the world beneath and above,— not giving and not getting; but drilling and getting; the pupils, because of the drilling, getting. He does not accumulate that they may accumulate. He sets them to accumulating from every source but himself.

"BABY STUDY."

G. Stanley Hall says : What we need are teachers. They must not be tyrants and their pupils henchmen, or the latter will lose their independence and finally become the slaves of political bosses upon reaching manhood. Schools must not be the place for developing what is syco-phantic and cringing. They must be controlled by the force that comes from knowledge. We know too little even of our own children. The time is coming when we will scrutinize and examine them as we do other spec-imens of natural history. Baby-study is, even now, being undertaken with great promise of results.

ELEMENTS IN TEACHING.

Prof. E. E. White says: The vital factor in teaching is the teacher. There are five elements in teaching. Con-trol comes first from power, which is inborn; then there is a perfect magnetism. The first element in teaching is good scholarship,—competency, which begets confidence on the part of the pupil; second, skill; third, heart-power, —love for the pupil, and love for the work; fourth, back-bone,—will-power,—a good article anywhere; it always tells in school. Manage a spirited boy as you would a spirited horse; keep a steady line and a still whip. Fifth, good eyes and good ears,—soul-sight; a blind teacher is at a great disadvantage in the government of children.)

LOVE FOR YOUR PUPILS.

From the *American Teacher* again, the following: Teachers, remember that a kind and encouraging word, especcially to the duller pupils, can never come amiss. Be chary of finding fault. If you can find anything in your pupils' work to commend you should commend it; if not, kindly and gently show him how to go about his work, then let him do it himself. Always strive to make the pupil understand the fact that he can do anything he undertakes, provided he will stick to it; and when he fails, do not scold, nor become impatient, but help him up and encourage him to try again.

Love your pupils and they will love you. Loving you they will strive to please you; and your rules, which would seem to them intolerably irksome did they dislike you, will become to them a source of pleasure in the fulfillment. If you wish to have an orderly school; if you wish to be happy in your work; if you wish your pupils to obey you and love you, *you must love them.* These three words applied in their full meaning would have prevented many a failure,—*love your pupils.*

A good, live teacher will do much toward overcoming surrounding difficulties. It is mind, after all, which is both the means and measure of success. There are true teachers in some schools, producing excellent results, with but limited appliances; there are others whose every want is supplied, producing inferior results. Considered purely as an investment, there is nothing that yields surer returns than a conscientious teacher with a talent for the work.

There is a constantly increasing demand upon our schools for results of greater commercial value. Teachers must consider these things.

USEFULNESS OF THE TEACHER.

This from the *New York School Journal:* Much of the usefulness of a teacher depends upon what his pupils think of him. Confidence, is back of influence, and respect behind confidence. This is just as much a law of nature as the law of chemical affinity. It would be as easy to overturn a mountain as to create confidence in a teacher, among pupils, who do not respect him.

The teacher who sits in his chair and dictates like a tyrant, or commands like a general, holding his pupils at arm's length, with a sort of '*don't-touch-me*' abhorrence, may succeed in making martinets, but his pupils will never become loving, useful, sympathetic men and women.

A well-educated man may be called a machine with a head and soul attachment. When the three elements are equally developed, the result is strength and love. The heartless disciplinarian leaves out the love, but cultivates the strength. But strength of body and mind, unless tempered with sympathy, is a dangerous union. Dynamite is strong; so were Jim Fisk and Bill Tweed; so were Nero and Napoleon.

APPEARANCE OF THE TEACHER.

The following as to qualities of the teacher is from a MR. O. B. BRUCE: Before his class the teacher should have due regard for his person, being becoming in his appearance, attitude and gesture; being cheerful, informed, and devoid of pedantry, or idiosyncrasies; being earnest, active and facile; being vigilant as to self, in tone, manner, patience, poise; as to pupil's answers, attention, and positions; as to temperature and ventilation of room, and the divisions of time for reviewing, imparting, testing and assigning work.

His language should be simple, precise, concise, and graphic; amply illustrated, yet devoid of diffuseness or glittering generalities.

WHY WE MIGRATE.

An article written by PROF. AARON GROVE, of Denver, contains some points of interest.

No small part of school troubles arise from misunderstandings caused by the teacher, and for which the teacher is chiefly responsible. Of hundreds of teachers now about folding their tents, many can find, upon reviewing the year's work, that some trivial and avoidable incidents have led to prejudices culminating in active opposition and positive enmity. In tracing causes of dissatisfaction, one usually finds that the school did no actual wrong; that the management was entitled to the full support of the authorities; yet there lurks about the affair an unexpected idea that a more judicious line of conduct might have averted the unsatisfactory issue.

Prejudice and enmity are frequently engendered against teachers and principals, especially during the first year of service, for slight and sometimes ridiculous causes. One's first year in a district is, for more than one reason, the critical and precarious one. The earnest and honest teacher who believes that the exact truth should be told, errs in saying to the mother of a boy, 'he is very dull of comprehension!' Suppose he is; it is not likely that the mother will believe it, and it is very likely that she will fail to appreciate the zeal that proclaims the fact. Failure to comprehend the relations of parent to child accounts for many a distressed hour of the teacher.

Writing notes to the home is a fruitful cause of misunderstanding. Only a master of the language can write a direct epistle without the probability of a reader's appropriating a meaning not intended by the writer. Notes are often misconstrued, and a little tempest caused thereby, when a personal interview would be sure to bring about the desired result. It is a cheap and easy thing to sit at one's desk and send to the home a note of complaint; the outcome is much safer and usually more effective if a visit be made to the house.

It is well known that true politeness is of the heart; however much may be there, the exterior should indicate its existence. 'You don't tell the truth!' 'You are ill-bred' taken alone are monstrous expressions to pass from teacher to pupil; but they do pass, and from those who ordinarily are ladies and gentlemen. Such expressions are buried in a mass of colloquial verbiage and not as emphatic as when the child repeats them at home, stripped of all modifying circumstances, so holds them up in all their unsightliness.

A compromising and consciliatory policy need never mean sacrifice of principle or dignity. One may be sensible of deep convictions, and yet not proclaim them upon unnecessary occasions. No power competent to direct successfully the district schools can lie in a purely *negative* character; but the evidences of a *positive* character need not necessarily be offensive. It has often been said of one of our old Illinois school-masters, who always made students, but who "migrated" yearly, until he left the profession, that 'he would cross a block and turn a corner for the purpose of treading on a man's toes.'

It sounds simple to write that it is unnecessary to tread on people's toes often, but, as I understand it, that is what causes the frequent changes of teachers in our schools.

PARAMOUNT PEDAGOGICAL PREREQUISITES

by JULIA A. PICKARD is an apt alliteration that I shall close the chapter with.

Probably no profession requires more skilled workers than that of teaching. To be fitted for the responsible duties, the teacher should posess:

First: Purity, that he may come before his pupils as a living example to them in thought, word, and deed; that his life may influence them to all that is good, and noble, and pure.

Second: Politeness, true and genuine, that he may have regard for the views and opinions of the little community over which he rules,

Third: Personal neatness, that he may appear before them in a creditable and becoming manner.

Fourth: Peculiar fitness for the work; pleasant, to attract instead of repel; patient, with faults and failings; pity in trivial trials and troubles; a physiognomist, to know how to deal with the different natures; a philanthropist, to exercise justice without favoritism.

Fifth: Preparation, by hard work, time, and thought, to be thoroughly qualified in all necessary studies; able to come before the classes master of the subject under discussion, instead of confined to text-books; knowing the how and why of methods and systems.

Sixth: Power to govern, not merely to quell revolts, and administer law, but to direct and guide the many wills in the proper channel, and, having done so, to hold them there.

Seventh: Punctuality, to be in the right place at the right time. If he must vary, better be too early than as many minutes late; having made a promise himself, keeping it, that he may expect and require the same of others.

Eighth: Practically, as only a few years, at most, is given to school-training; therefore pupils should be taught what is needed to make them thoughtful, earnest men and women to contend successfully with the realities of life.

Ninth: Personally, having a firm belief of what is right, an object to be attained, and following his own course carefully and to a successful issue, instead of wavering and altogether losing himself in another's way and method.

Tenth: Pluck. Don't become discouraged because unappreciated, but perseveringly, persistently, pertinaciously press on, and success will ultimately crown your effort.

CHAPTER III.

POINTS IN THE FORMER CHAPTER CONTRASTED,— TEACHERS' FOLLIES,—ADMONITIONS AND CRITICISMS.

TALKING TOO MUCH.

In a school journal styled the *Moderator*, · published in Michigan, a few years ago, a writer signing himself 'Pedagogue' gives vent to the following: How many teachers we find who talk almost constantly to their pupils when not hearing a recitation, thinking this the only sure way of securing attention and government.   This is especially true with teachers who have a great many rules, so many in fact, that they themselves almost forget, till they have gone over them, at least once a day, before their school for two weeks.

Such teachers are guilty of cannonading their pupils with orders like these: "Take down your hand, sir." "Turn round in your seat, James."   "Sit up, Mary." "Attention, Susan."   "John, did I not say no more leaving seats?"   Etc., etc.

These are *commands*, and the wise teacher will never even make a *request*, when a suggestion will accomplish the purpose.   They appeal to instincts which are slumbering, and to motives, which, so far as they are concerned, have no existence.

Then, again, time taken up talking to pupils takes time from their studies, and interferes with the progress of their work.   But, here, the teacher seems to think that the pupil can listen to a scolding and get a lesson well at the same time.   This of course, after a time, become monotonous to the pupil, who soon manifests a disinterestedness. Then, failure to interest fails to instruct.

The lecture system in recitations will fail of its purpose for the very same reasons. Pupils may receive instruction under this system, and still have little or no idea of the subject, never having been called upon to express themselves. Thus one of the main objects of the recitation, viz. power and habit of correct oral expression, is lost to the pupil.   .   .   .   .

TEACHERS DON'T READ ENOUGH.

The following from the *Iowa Teacher.* Most teachers do not read enough. They do not realize how much help they could get from good books relating to their profession. They worry along through an entire term with a few vexatious questions of teaching or school management, when a few hours reading might clear up all difficulties. Teachers frequently lose positions, or are unable to get any except the most unsatisfactory ones, when by the careful study of two or three books, they could so improve themselves as to be able to secure good positions. Economy in preparation is extravagance in results both in financial and educational points of view.

HOBBY HORSE SYSTEM.

ANNA C. BRACKETT says: We have to guard continually against the two extremes to which school-work ever has tendencies,— the *riding of a hobby* and *the moving in a rut.* The hobby-horse system is the one in which guiding lines ought to be tense, and steadily held, but at the same time, lightly. Each mind must be felt, but no one pushed or pulled; the entire class as a whole must be worked smoothly and harmoniously together,—moving on in a right line, or rounding a curve with caution, yet with safety.

COMPARISONS.

In an editorial column of the *Educational Weekly*, this language occurs: "Comparisons are oderous," quoth Mrs. Malaprop (meaning odious). And this sentiment of the old lady, albeit her memory of words was defective, finds an echo in every human breast.

There is nothing we so generally and cordially detest as comparisons,—if they do not show us off to the best advantage. It is the nature of a comparison, obviously, to add to the advantage or praise of one by what it takes from another, and thus it is so purely a one-sided affair that it is altogether tabooed in polite society.

Some teachers in trying to stimulate a dull or lagging pupil, compare him to one who stands higher in his class. This is a most objectionable method. It is certain to make the one pupil bitter and angry, and the other intolerably vain. The slow pupil would be more than human if he were not aroused to hate his more successful school-mate, while the brighter one can hardly resist the temptation to be conceited, and look down with scorn upon others. Especially bad is the effect when the teacher draws comparisons of this kind before the whole school.

Teachers, themselves, would find it especially disagreeable to be thus singled out for an object of especial remark, disparaging or complimentary. Then one thing certain, children instead of being less sensitive than their elders are usually more so. Hence the shrewdness of Mrs. Malaprop's remark.

"TOO MANY THINGS,"

is from the same source.

There is a tendency in our day to attempt the teaching of far too many things in our schools. There seems to be a general impression that with the constant enlargement of the province of knowledge, the curriculum of the schools should be enlarged to correspond. But there is a decided limit to possibilities in this direction.

So much of the knowledge that has been given to the world of late years has been the result of the study of specialists, that it is folly for a general student to attempt to master a tithe of it. Much more absurd, then, is it to expect to teach this tithe or less in the common schools, and more, it is not the mission of the common schools to attempt such a thing.

Our schools should teach a few things thoroughly, and by so doing arouse in the young a desire for more extended study. A few—a very few subjects well understood, as far as the pupil has progressed in them, are far better than numberless topics merely touched upon. Do not try to teach pupils *too much*, but teach everything that is taught with the utmost thoroughness. Duty is not accomplished by simply informing the young minds on this or that topic; but in endeavoring to interest them in the acquisition of knowledge, and in training and developing their faculties so that future study will be not only profitable, but pleasant to them.

WHAT SHOULD BE MEMORIZED.

ADA A. AHLBORN writes: Very much of the knowledge contained in our text-books ought to be so marked for the benefit of those teachers who think every line in fine print ought to be memorized, that they could not be mistaken as to what to teach and what to leave out. Memory is kinder to us than such teachers, and so soon excuses us from the task of retaining unimportant matter. Recently I heard a pupil say, "You are the first teacher who did not require us to commit every table in compound numbers."

Of course all the principal tables were committed; but what if they do *not* know that 120 wine gallons make a pipe of Teneriffe; that 28 pounds make a bushel of oats in Connecticut, and 32 in California? What if they *never* learn to give the old stereotyped answer, Mt. Everest is the highest mountain peak in the world? Who cares? These things are to be found by reference to the book and not to the memory.

With the best training there is only a certain amount of knowledge that the mind can contain, and, if we fill it up with petty tables, dates, islands, mountain peaks, etc., etc., it must be at the expense of crowding out what is more valuable.

Teachers should discern this truth,—yet, *teachers' examinations* very often consist of the kind of knowledge not to be committed.

For instance, this question, given at an examination: Give the population and area of each state(?) Truly, an applicant could give no better evidence of incompetency to teach, than a correct answer to such a question. It would almost certainly prove an attention to trifles and details to the neglect of broader and more important truths and principles.

The teacher must decide upon the important points of each lesson, and these mastered, should be sufficient. If we group too many little facts about a *great truth*, the pupils lose sight of *it*, in their endeavor to master details. Fix principles and we might almost promise in scripture language, "That all other things will be added thereto."

HOW TO IMPROVE ONE'S METHODS,

by PROF. JOHN OGDEN, applies the '*reductio ad absurdum*.'

He says: Do not subscribe for an educational paper; or if you do, don't read it. Don't hesitate, however, to borrow your neighbor's journal under the pretense that you are going to subscribe for it. Don't attend any teachers' institutes, or educational .meetings of any kind in your county, and be sure you do not go beyond its limits to find one elsewhere. Don't study or read anything except the branches you are expected to teach; and make it a point to study those as little as possible.

Proceed on the supposition that you know all about teaching that is worth knowing; and to be consistent stick to that plan. Don't buy any books on teaching, unless it be those with questions and answers, ready cut and dried. Be sure, in case you do invest, that you buy those in which the questions and answers both are short and easy. You can find such not far away.

Be independent. Stick to the old traditions. Teach as your fathers taught. Don't be wheedled into any of the '*new-fangled notions.*'

In short, illustrate, as far as you can, your own ignorance, by denying that there is any such thing as a science of education, or if there is, that you know anything about it.

Make strenuous efforts to know nothing except the little—*that you do not know how to teach.*

Illustrate this by your strict adherence to printed rules. The more inconsistent the better. It shows great faith in authorship.

And lastly,—*teach cheap.* Don't insist on receiving more pay for taking charge of the children of a neighborhood, than a young man does, who takes care of sheep. For *your* services probably will not be half so valuable as *his.*

These rules followed out with care and you will cer-tainly *succeed*—in making a dunce of yourself, and in leading as many others to follow your example as have not sense enough to do otherwise.

is from the *New England Journal of Education.*

No reform in school life has been more fruitful of good results, than the change from "hearing lessons" to genuine oral instruction.

But every forward movement in education is dogged by a group of caricatures, exaggerations, and imitations, which threaten to overwhelm it, and often do postpone its true influence.

Among these caricatures of oral instruction none is more mischievous than the habit of inordinate talking by the teacher, who confounds it with an interminable pouring forth of useful information by word of mouth.

This is the most dangerous abuse because the most common. An untrained teacher is not easily routed from the notion that instruction consists in pouring the contents of a book into the mind of a child. If forbidden this use of the book a teacher of this description naturally falls back upon the next position, which is to fill her own mind with the contents of the volume, and retail it in speech for the benefit of her class. Of course, this is not oral teaching in any sense of the term. It is rather the worst form of book teaching. . . . .

Certainly, the author of a good text-book will condense, arrange and study a suitable method of presenting the matter he desires to impart. But an untrained teacher will surely not improve on this presentation, but will so dilute the author's statement, in dispensing it, as to rob it of its chief value and increase the difficulty of the pupils. . . . A great deal of this sort of teaching may be classified as information and twaddle,—the hazy, inconsequential, sometimes ungrammatical flood of words that inundates the weary class, as effectially drowning the information imported, as a gallon of tepid water will strangle the most fragrant cup of tea.

The disease was well hit off by an afflicted little boy who came to his mother at the close of the first day of school with the plaint,—"O, mother, I am tired to death; the new teacher *talks so much with her mouth.*" Just that, the interminable gabble that comes from no deeper place than the mouths or the shallows of a vacant mind, flooded with gossip and words, is the curse of thousands of schoolrooms. Perhaps this last stage of false teaching is worse than the first. It is possible that a child, by dint of storing the memory with the well-selected periods of a good text-book, may sometime awake to a realizing sense of their contents and find himself possessed of valuable information. But it is doubtful if even the elastic mind of childhood is capable of wrestling with the flood of talk with which the devoted class is so often deluged. . . . There is danger that this sort of teaching will greatly hinder the results of the new educational methods. . .
The object lesson has become a nuisance in thousands of schools where the young graduate from the Normal has simply recited *her* lesson from her notebook, and told her children what to say. And there is a great danger, especially in the classes in literature, history, philosophy and kindred studies, that the pupil will be cheated by his right of individual acquisition, compelled to be one of an audience listening to a daily drizzle of talk, with occasional interruptions of a hurried answer during the pauses.

Young graduates regard the slow gait of the average school-boy and the flighty mental condition of the average school-girl as positive torture. Hence the habit of inordinate talk is thus formed as a refuge from what seems the stupidity of the pupil or even from a conscientious desire to do something in the recitation hour. But nowhere is self-restraint so needful, humility so precious, judicious silence so golden, as in the presence of a class of children making their first essay at climbing the hill of knowledge.

PUPILS CAN'T REMEMBER EVERYTHING.

An unknown author gives us the following: It is a mistake to attempt to demand that pupils remember permanently everything they learn. Of course they do not, cannot do it, and to attempt to demand it is absurd.

The true idea is to have them carefully taught everything that is taught, pausing in the teaching and studying until certain that they have digested it, and after that endeavoring to secure the remembrance, for ready use, the leading thought which is likely to recall the details in case of an emergency. Essential for permanency, details for dessert.

TEACHERS ARE NOT FAULTLESS.

Again, these words: It is vain for a teacher to attempt to pass for a faultless character in the eyes of his pupils. He is not faultless and never can succeed in so far deceiving his pupils as to make them believe he is. He who would reach the human heart must himself be human; and the most human thing in human nature is imperfection.

LOSING CONTROL OF SCHOOL.

From the *New York School Journal*, the following "Nine Rules for Losing Control of School" certainly come under the head of "Teachers' Follies:"

Neglect to furnish each pupil plenty of suitable seat-room. Make commands that you do not nor can not see executed. Be frivolous and joke pupils to such an extent that they will feel called upon to "talk back." Or be so cold and formal as to repel them. Allow them to find out that they can annoy you. Promise more in your pleasant moods than you can perform, and threaten more in your blue spell than you intend to perform. Be so variable in your moods that what was allowable yesterday is criminal to-day, or *vice versa*. Be overbearing to one class of pupils and obsequious to another. Utterly ignore the little formalities and courtesies of life in the treatment of pupils in school and elsewhere. Consider the body, mind, and soul of a child utterly unworthy of study and care.

WASTING TIME.

A quotation from the language of PROF. DOTY, of Chicago, shows up a number of follies:

"Twenty ways of wasting time." Stopping work to attend to individual cases of discipline. Waiting for dilatory scholars. Lecturing or talking upon matters of little importance. Fussy and indirect ways of beginning work. Slow and noisy movements of pupils about the room. Inadequate preparation for recitation. Writing letters or working upon records during session hours. Permitting irrelevant questions by pupils. Permitting pointless corrections by pupils. Wandering from the subject-matter of recitation. Speaking too slowly. Speaking in such a manner as to disturb and distract pupils at their work. Putting work upon slates, paper, or blackboard too slowly. Having no definite order of procedure in a recitation. Tolerating habits of slowness or laziness in some pupils. Dwelling upon what pupils already know. Repetition of answers or parts of answers. Permitting such inattention as to require repetition of questions. Failure of some pupils to understand each step in a recitation. Having no well-defined *next* upon which to direct effort.

ON FUSSINESS.

There is occasionally a fussy soul, who is continually troubling himself about things of no account. If he is in church he is trying to find out: "Of what kind of dust Adam was created," and, "how the star in the East can be reconciled with astronomical facts."

If he is trying to be in business, he will spend much time in computing exactly "how long it would take a cent at compound six per cent. interest to amount to a million of dollars," or, "what the national debt would have amounted to if the war had continued a year and six months longer."

If he is teaching, he is puzzling and boring everybody by his impracticable questions in reference to absolutely unimportant and unprofitable subjects, such as, "How many of the plays of Shakespeare were written during the last two years of his life?" "Who was the first man to whom Columbus suggested the possibility of finding a new route to India?" "Can an adverb modify prepositions?" "What great man was born with a wart on the end of his little finger of the left hand?" He will kindly suggest to you in a sort of pedantic way, that "the generally accepted pronunciation of *dē'pot* is depot, accented on the first syllable," and that you "inadvertently said mū'seum instead of muse'um." He will look wondrous wise and imagine that you are mightily impressed with his erudition, and that you are profoundly thankful for his suggestions. Such a person has his place but it is a remarkably small one.

FROM CONFESSIONS OF A SCHOOL-MASTER:

Read by HON. M. A. NEWELL of Maryland before a body of educators: Abstract.

Among the things confessed were a fondness for hobbies and an inclination to ride them to death; sins of

—not ignorance of arithmetic, grammar nor even the ome-tries and ologies,—but of something still more important, —ignorance of the nature of the boys and girls to whom this knowledge is to be imparted; ignorance of their intel-lectual natures, of their moral natures, of their emotional natures; a want of staying power; for though we run well we get out of breath too soon.

We require to be wound up so often, some of us every year, some every three years, except superintendents, who run on an average of four years.

DRIVING.

Still another anonymous point: An old doctor of divinity once said: Gentlemen, remember that a man is somewhat like a hog; rub the bristles the right way and he is contented, but the wrong way and he squeals.   The teacher whose main object before his class is to *make them learn*, is rubbing the bristles the wrong way.   *There is'nt a particle of moral virtue in driving.*   Good may possibly come of it, — somehow, somewhere, sometime, — but seldom. Look out for the driving teacher!   There is a screw loose somewhere.   The foreman who gets the best work out of his men, says "Come" not "Go."   There is very little good public opinion in a school that is driven.   It may be orderly, quiet, famous for good *recitations*, but there is no heart in it.   Nine-tenths of the whole school will rejoice in a good trick nicely done.   Respect, consciousness, moral character, true scholarship, any or all of the virtues can not be driven into scholars.   *Never!*   It is not possible to drive a boy and make a good man of him.

DONT'S.

Miss ALICE M. BURNEY, of Geneva, Ohio, gives a short chapter of "Don'ts:"

Don't scold continually or for every little, trifling offense; "familiarity breeds contempt," — so your pupils will soon come to think that scolding is your forte, and that you do it for fun. Thus, its effect, when deserved, is lost.

Don't attempt to teach by comparison until you weigh well that the minds of children are easily confused; and if you attempt to teach the correct by showing the incorrect, you run the risk of impressing upon them the very thing you seek to eradicate.

Don't try to have your pupils learn too many things, or spend your strength in advancing them too rapidly. You might as well "pour water through a sieve."

Don't forget that your pupils are rational beings, and that they have a code of rights that should be respected as sacredly as those of their elders.

Don't forget that your pupils are the men and women of to-morrow; that they are essentially what they are made by precept and example; and that to primary pupils example is of more value than precept.

Don't think that order consists in the quiet of the tomb, or fancy that the air of an Egyptian mummy is creditable in a child.

And, finally, don't forget to look and be your brightest, sweetest and prettiest, when in the presence of your pupils.

CHAPTER IV.

MORALS, AND THE INSTRUCTION THEREOF.

OUTSIDE INFLUENCES.

A quotation from Supt. Edgerly, of Fitchburg, Mass., is used at the beginning of this chapter. He says: There are many influences outside the school room affecting the progress of the pupils. The home training is seen in the work of the school room. The way in which the time of the pupil is spent has much to do with this work. That time may be so spent as to be very demoralizing to pupils, unfitting them for their daily tasks.

Mentally and physically the pupil is weakened or strengthened by the books he reads outside, by his companions, by his conversation at home, on the street, on the play-grounds. Thus, the school is only *one* of the many influences tending to shape character. We are too much inclined to speak of the school as the only agent at work moulding the character of youth. The fact that a boy or girl, a young man or young woman has attended this school or that school, this college or that college, does not of itself imply that the education is good or poor. We lay too much stress upon this. Pupils begin to attend school at the age of five or six. The majority do not attend after they are fourteen. Under the most favorable circumstances the child is at school a little more than half the days of the year. The schools, however, are responsible for much, and every one connected with their management must be made to feel that responsibility. The schools should work in harmony with other influences for good.

RELIGIOUS TEACHING

Rev. Mr. Frisbie said before a gathering of Iowa educators: All specially religious text-books are put away. There can be no religious machinery brought to bear at the public expense. The state is not an evangelist. Very well. There is nothing left to produce moral impressions. The State does not specify them. It says, "I want intelligence." The way is clear for the living teacher to lead the sparkling hosts of children by the sweet springs of truth. He may not preach; he may not evangelize; but it may shine out from his face that truth is better than lies; that a reverent spirit abhors profanity; that temperance and virtue hold an inalienable right in the human soul; and, until it shall be shown that there *is no divine power or person*, it will be no breach of honor for him to let it be understood that before the Creator he walks with a subdued, receptive soul. The Book, every book of creeds and forms, goes out. The living teacher, a living epistle, to be read and understood, even by the child, come in."

MORAL TRAINING.

The following appeared in a recent number of the *New York School Journal*: It is not possible to arrange a purely intellectual system of instruction without a particle of moral training in it. Morality cannot be divorced from the teaching of arithmetic. It is absolute folly to teach that religion is one thing and business or education another. Read the Bible. This is right. The ten commandments. They are right. The Lord's prayer. Nothing better. But all these are not religion. When work begins, then practical religion begins. An angry scowl on a teacher's face will knock all devotional feelings out of a school in less than a "*A tenth of a second.*" Who would hear a preacher preach, who is a saint in the pulpit, but a Satan out of it? What is a teacher's moral teaching good for, if he keeps his morality between Bible covers? We want everything great and good in the school-room, but we do not want it assigned as an opening exercise. It is not claimed that Christ's sermon on the mount was introduced by reading the Scriptures, singing, and prayer. He went up into the mount and when He was set His disciples came to Him and He taught them. What taught them? His words? Yes, somewhat. But what would have been those majestic words without his life? Tell us, ye sticklers of long prayers, made for a pretense, at the opening of a school. Children are taught by living, tangible objects. Sermons to children, *good for anything*, are almost as rare as orange trees in Manitoba.

Let us have living, walking, talking, loving, Christian actions in school teachers, and all else will take care of itself. The teaching of the facts of religion are far more intimately connected with success in life than the teaching of any of the arts or sciences.

What is religion? Here are few of its foundations: There is a God. The principles of His government are just. He sees and knows us. We are accountable to Him. We know what is right and wrong. We voluntarily choose to do what we please. When we do wrong we suffer for it. When we do right we are made happy (always, forsooth?). We should obey the golden rule. We should do right because it is right. We should love what is pure, lovely, good, kind, and benevolent, and hate what is impure, hateful, evil, unkind and malevolent. These principles can be taught everywhere and always. Many can go further and teach the Bible and the church. But all teachers, everywhere and always can and should teach religion.

MORAL INSTRUCTION.

Some extracts from an address by Prof. J. T. Hand, of Texas, are very pointed.

The address was delivered at Gainesville, Texas, during the session of a summer normal school.

It is not to discuss the Bible in the schools. It is not Christianity against Judaism. It is not Protestantism against Romanism. Nor Calvinism against Armenianism. It is morality—simple, pure, fundamental. Morality? What is morality, moral teaching, obligation to law? *Morality is the doctrine or practice of the duties of life.*

The need of such teaching is self evident. There can be no such thing as training without it; no mental development which brings the person not to this line. All growth must increase the responsibilities. Duties increase as life unfolds and knowledge comes.

Moral teaching shows one's relations to these duties. It is in respect to the duties of life that every lesson, in all the school days, is learned and recited. To teach a pupil how to speak and write a language is one phase of preparation. To teach that the pupil should speak and write the truth is the moral part of the instruction. The former without the latter is worse than speechless ignorance.

The light which reveals the right way to any place or thing, will surely discover to the traveler all the by-ways and pit falls. Morality shows the propriety and necessity of walking in the highway, instead of wading the slough, simply to see how deep the mud is and where one will come out. Let this suffice for definitions.

How to teach. No instruction will influence to action without the force of authority like a cyclone behind it. If you say, "You must do this," it is incumbent upon you to show "Why ought I." The 'oughtness' of the thing is the point. How are you to teach that you ought to do right, is more important than how he may know what is right. God in every soul speaks the eternal word of law.

One way is to repeat over and over that the church says this or that is so; therefore you ought. Another is to say "The Bible says so." "This has been the practice of respectable people for generations past, and you ought to do as other people; because they probably are right, and then, it is customary or fashionable. All these are wrong. The latter especially. It is the supremest jibberism.

If you give the book, or church, or society as authority, you will have to go back to the question of genuineness, and finally find that the authority which commands this back of all, but still under both the church and the Bible.

The child is the offspring of nature; show that oughtness is everywhere in the "nature of things" and you will not only strike the root of the matter, but reach the roots of the beings you address.

Do unto others as you would that others should do unto you, is so much an instinct that no child's mind is so obtuse as not to bow in submission to its divinity. Begin, I say, on the plane of nature, keep the self-evident truths of God that teach the duties of life ever before the pupil, by the practice of morality yourself and by often pointing out their application in the every day life of the pupil.

To reiterate precepts by the week, month or year, unless the fountain is bursting forth from your own heart, will be like laboring at a pump handle where there is no water. I do not depreciate reading or memorizing scripture precepts, yet they are but the declaration of results.

The solution of the problem is in the heart and soul. Get at the heart. . . . But to the question as it relates to the interests of the child while a pupil under

your care: It is better for the government of the school.
Their is no governing children nor men without morality.
The rules of the duties of the school, duties to self, to
others and to the teacher, — these duties observed, will
create a mental and moral habit that will extend to the
other duties in the home life and afterward to business life
and social intercourse.

As to the methods of moral teaching, would I be mis-
understood if I say, first: You should have no method.
That is, no stereotyped rule as to time and form of lecture.
Surely never administer a dose of *ethics* as a punishment
or revenge upon a pupil. Never! never!

If they are to have it daily, weekly, or monthly, they
will prepare for the affliction, like the boy who put a blacksmith's apron under his coat, and thus they will defeat
your purpose, be it ever so good.

The times and seasons will come when "words fitly
spoken shall be like apples of gold in pictures of silver."
For a soft answer turneth away wrath. No set time
should be given out. Make your own arrangements as to
time and matter. Be fully prepared to say the right thing
in the right way. But you need not advertise it. A good
thing will keep until used; so bide your time; speak only
such things as you know to be true and useful, and those
you believe and live yourself. Let the form of the lecture
be not all formal, stereotyped, dogmatic, and cold. Better
not speak at all unless your heart speaks. If one pupil or
class needs teaching on a special point, don't bring him or
them into contempt by personal rebuke. Tell them their
faults alone, and show them the true way. Do not put
off a duty indefinitely through modesty or caution. Be
heroic. *Have the courage of your convictions.*

But you can do nothing without thinking out a plan

for yourself. No other person's method will do you. David could not fight in Saul's armor.

Arrange what you want to teach in proper order; begin at the beginning; be systematic, logical, natural. For example, you determine to teach this month some practical morals: You can classify them somewhat after this order: Our duty to ourselves—self-culture. Our duty toward our fellowmen. Our duties to God—piety.

MORAL EDUCATION.

The following on "Moral Education" taken from the *Teachers' Institute,* was probably written by COL. F. W. PARKER. First, what is meant by moral education? And second, how can it be carried on? In the minds of many it is supposed to be effected by reading in the Bible, and remarks about lying, stealing, and profanity; and so the teacher works aimlessly and often vainly. It is as difficult to educate morally as it is intellectually. Probably far more so. If moral education can be explained, it is possible for the teacher to learn how to carry it on.

A young man is in a bank; there are around him many dollars lying unguarded; he is tempted to take some of them for his own use; but does not do it. Here we say is a moral act. A moral act is one where right and wrong are concerned. We know, we feel, and we choose. This distinction in our mental acts is very old. I know that the sun is up; this is intellect. I experience love for my mother; this is feeling. I choose to go to Boston rather than Philadelphia; this is willing. All mental acts are one or the other of these. It is not right or wrong to know about the sun, or to love my mother. But the choosing of one thing when the other should have been selected, may be wrong. Moral actions, then, pertain to the will—the choosing power.

When we choose, we do so from certain motives. The young bank clerk was influenced by some motive. He was afraid of being discovered, or felt that it would be degrading to him, or some other motive. An individual who chooses right things instead of wrong ones, acts morally upright.

Look at the clerk once more. He has money by him. He may take it or he may leave it alone. He leaves it alone, and we ask him what induced him to this choice. We find that he has been brought up to know that this is right. Then he is ·intelligent on right or wrong. We find that he has followed such a course ever since he was a boy. Then he has formed the habit of choosing to do the right act. We find that there is associated in his mind pleasure in choosing to do right, and pain if he chooses the wrong.

Whoever will morally educate a person, must see that he acts from proper motives. Make him intelligent, form good habits in him, and associate pleasure with right-doing. Suppose the child who comes to the teacher is what is known as a good child. Let us ask why he is good. The answer is, his parents have morally educated him. How? They have made him understand what right-doing is; have insisted on his doing those acts until he formed the habit; and, finally, caused him to be happy in doing these acts. The little boy is told, for example, not to do a certain thing, say, for instance, not to eat an apple. He learns by his mother's face, even before he can understand her words, that the act of eating the apple must not be chosen. He refrains and sees the look of pleasure on his mother's face. This is repeated, almost hourly, for many years, and makes a deep impression. As he grows older, by reasoning with him a ground of intelligence is laid, why he should always choose the right. In all these years he is forming a habit of doing or not doing, –that is, choosing or not choosing; and, also, fixing in his mind, powerful associations as to choosing the good or preferring the bad. As soon as possible he should learn the consequences of right-doing and wrong-doing. He tells a lie. His father shows him that he cannot tell when to believe him. He tells the truth and he learns that he gains the confidence and good will of his father. By the steady pressure of natural consequences of his acts his intelligence is cultivated; his understanding connects cause and effect; he sees that there is a moral law.

A teacher in one of the lower wards of New York city, had a class of boys who habitually told lies and stole. He told an anecdote to them one day of a boy who was alone in the office of his employer, and the money drawer stood open, and yet that he did not take anything from it. "He was a great fool," said one of the boys. To cite the moral law, or to express horror at this remark, he felt would do no good. He quietly replied, "I think not." He then portrayed the return of the employer, his finding his money all safe; and that he had done it as a trial; that it led to increased confidence in the boy, and to his advancement. In this way the teacher addressed the intelligence of his pupils. They saw that right acts led to desirable consequences.

The plan of the teacher should be mapped out. He should proceed as systematically as he does to train the intellect.

There are, first, duties which the pupil owes to himself: viz., *self-control*, which forbids or covers intemperance, licentiousness, ambition, vanity, covetousness, jealousy false-honor and gambling. Second, *self-culture* which demands attention to diet, dress, exercise, cleanliness, taste, science and morality.

Then there are duties to others; viz., respect, kindness, courtesy, honesty, reciprocity, charity and gratitude. This relation to others forbids hard-heartedness, insolence, peevishness, arrogance, scorn, ridicule, vulgarity, assault, defrauding, slander and censoriousness.

Instead of classifying an act, the teacher should, as a practical matter, prefer to employ maxims that may be easily learned. .Thus, he need not say, "Such an act is slander and is wrong." Or, "So and so is profane and vulgar." But use his maxims. For self-control, "Do thyself no harm." For self-culture, "Secure a complete self-development." "Grow in kindness." "Grow in wisdom." "Love the bright and beautiful," etc. For duties towards others. "Do good to all mankind as you have opportunity." "Give to the poor." "Be thankful." "Deal justly." "Love your neighbor." "Respect authority," etc.

The moral principles involved in an act of wrong-doing by a pupil should be discussed by the teacher in the presence of the pupil before a punishment is inflicted. And often the effect of such a course will justify the teacher in withholding the punishment. To illustrate: Suppose John has Henry's pencil and refuses to return it. He says: "I found it." The teacher asks, "If we lose a pencil do we still own it?" Say this before the school. The school answers, "Yes, sir." "Whose pencil is this, then?" "Henry's." "Should John want to keep Henry's property?" "No, sir." "Why not?" "It is wrong." "What is the rule?" "Love your neighbor." "Would John be happy if he kept Henry's pencil?" Etc., etc.

Suitable anecdotes could here be related. The boy who wrongfully claimed the pencil will readily assent to the claim of the other.

Suppose one boy is over-bearing and is guilty of striking smaller boys. A case comes before the teacher. He states the case to all the pupils. They listen. The teacher says, "I saw William crying, and learned that Thomas struck him. It was not an accident. Thomas says that William called him names. Should William have called him names?" "No, sir!" "Why not?" "Be courteous," one pupil says. "Is that the maxim?" "Do good to your neighbor," says another. "Was William made happy?" "No, sir." "Why not?" "It is not doing good to your neighbor." "Should Thomas have struck William, then?" "No, sir." "Why not?" "Because he was not doing good to his neighbor." "Was William or Thomas either made happier by it?" "No, sir." "Thomas gratified his passions as a dog gratifies himself by biting a man who speaks to him. He is larger and stronger than William. Would he have struck William if he had thought William would overcome him?" "No, sir." What is such conduct called?" "Cowardice." "Are cowards loved and respected? Or do they make others happy?" "No, sir." "Then, you see, one wrong thing leads to another. When William called Thomas names, he should have waited till William's ill-temper subsided. Then he could have said 'William, you did not do right in calling me names.' William would certainly have made some apology; but if he did not, Thomas should then have brought the matter before me. I hope William will apologize, yet, and then I am sure Thomas will do the same, for his conduct." Etc., etc.

Then again, there are very few pupils who will not acknowledge a wrong act when taken in private. In fact, this is one of the most wholesome and effective means of breaking pupils off from vicious habits. They will confess privately that they have done wrong. And although they may do so again, yet each confession of the kind made to a warm-hearted, sympathetic teacher weakens the tendency towards vice and strengthens the better powers of the moral nature, just as a repetition of the blow of a wood-chopper tends to make of him an expert axman. It is so in all the performances demanded of a human being. Repetition of the act, gives the power and insures a more perfect performance the next time. It matters not whether it be a mental or a physical act. Then a bad boy should have an opportunity to perform a good act, if it be no more than a confession of his guilt. And he will do this in private, if rightly managed, and, that too, without having it wrung from him by a coercive act on the part of his teacher. In fact, it must come out free as a fountain gushing from the hillside, in order to produce the impression desired. Then as soon as the confession is offered to the teacher, thus, in private, if he be skillful he can then and there turn the whole matter to account for the future good of that pupil. If deftly managed, a vicious boy will go away after a private interview, full of friendship and respect for his teacher. Then a long step in the right direction has been taken. The teacher has a tenacious hold on him for the future, and may succeed in making a radical change in his conduct. He who punishes an infraction of rules without discussing the moral principles, either privately or publicly, loses the opportunity to give his pupils moral training. They are enlightened by discussion. . . . .

MORALITY TAUGHT BY INFLUENCE.

Prof. G. W. Hoenshel says upon "Moral Education."
. . . . Right living is of more importance than mere knowledge, for there is such a thing as an educated villain.

Children are not naturally entirely good, nor are they wholly evil. If prompted by right motives they will discard vice and choose virtue. The training in morals is not accomplished by the teacher alone, but he can do much in arousing the sleeping energies of the soul. Words are indeed powerful, but in moral education they are not so mighty as actions. But little good can ever be accomplished by giving to pupils, lectures on morality. It is the *silent* influence of the surroundings that will form character. Truth and beauty are everywhere associated together, and what is beautiful can not be far from being good.. For this reason the school-room should be pleasant. A dreary school-room is not favorable to a growth of morality. It should be the most cheerful place in the community. What incentives to right action in bare walls and gloomy windows? A child who is taught to appreciate the true and beautiful in nature, art, and literature, will strive after the beautiful in character, and can not be far from right. Such are the teachings of nature.

The *influence of the teacher* is a prominent factor in moral training. Children imitate the actions of their superiors, and, strange as it may seem, they copy vices in preference to virtues. The teacher exerts a silent influence over his pupils for good or for evil, and this influence is but the reflection of his own character. All exert this influence; then how careful should the teacher be, that it is for good. Better have *no* school than one taught by an immoral teacher, for the influence he exerts upon the minds of the pupils for evil will over-balance the good he may accomplish by developing the intellect. The conclusion, then, is, that all teachers should be positive moral men and women.

By these external influences,—pleasant surroundings

and a good teacher,—much can be accomplished. Those who talk the most about morality have not the greatest claims to success as teachers of morality. It is the *living model* that conquers, not directly, but indirectly. Many incidents occur during the day by which a moral lesson may be taught. The wise teacher will take advantage of every opportunity to impress a moral truth. It *can not be done by lecturing*, for a talk on duty is, of all things, most distasteful. It is the word fitly spoken, at the proper time, that is impressed upon the mind of the child. But still more depends upon the teacher behind the word than upon any thoughts uttered.

Teach morality indirectly by history and biography. The life of every noted man contains a moral lesson, or many. Let pupils search for them. Talk of the causes of war, and the motives which prompted heroes to do deeds of valor. Pupils will soon distinguish between noble and ignoble acts. In teaching morality it is not necessary to teach sectarianism.

What is needed is a knowledge of the principles of morality and the rules of action that will lead to success in life. This is the foundation upon which all may build, but the structure will depend upon the taste of the individual.

CHAPTER V.

GENERAL HINTS AND DIRECTIONS.

ANNA C. BRACKETT in a kind of a general way says some good things in the following :

Where there are schools there must be text-books, and where there are text-books there must be publishers. But because there are publishers, is it necessary that we use every kind of text-book in a series? It seems to me that these series of books on the same subject are one of the most assidious evils in our schools.

Readers must be graded, and carefully, too; but it does not follow that every thing must be graded. There is sense in giving the child, at first, maps with only the general outline of the continent and the principal rivers and mountains, and not confusing his eye with the innumerable details, which ought to be left until later in the course, and most of which ought never to be given at all. But the equator remains persistently the equator, and can not be simplified. It is no easier to learn its definition from a small quarto with a picture on the outside than from a large octavo. If the idea can be grasped once for all, when that time comes it should be given.

These series of geographies and of arithmetics as well, have their most striking success in dulling and stupefying the minds of the children who are so unfortunate as to have them. It is especially of arithmetic that I want to speak, however.

I venture to express the thought that too much time is

spent on examples of very simple numbers when the same
practice might be secured by longer numbers and something practical learned at the same time. For instance,
when children are adding, why may they not just as well
perform examples consisting of three or four numbers of
five or six figures each, as to add, simply, orally? And I
should not stop at sums which do not exceed nine. If you
do not make any difficulty about setting down the *three*
and saving the *seven* (the answer being seventy-three), the
child will find no difficulty. One will accept this as naturally as he accepts the house he lives in. But if you stop
him to state that ten units make ten and that seventy-
three units equal seven tens and three units, and that he
must set down his three units and save his seven tens for
the column of tens,—then he loses his way and gets tired
because he does not understand. Few people realize how
short sentences must be, in order that the child's mind
may hold them. The general trouble when a child does
not understand, is that like old Father Taylor, of Boston,
he "has lost track of his *Nominative Case.*"

The child of seven has not reached the stage of relative
pronouns or conjunctive adverbs. Let him work simply.
Take it for granted that he can do a simple thing in a
simple way and he will do it. Confuse and aggravate his
mind with long explanations, and he becomes worried and
disgusted. Let him have real examples in addition on his
slate. Teach him to set his examples down properly and
neatly, to rule his lines straight, and to put his figures in
straight rows. All this is work that ought to be done at
first. But it cannot be done if he is kept on real work.
Never mind about the "tens and units column" rigmarole.
Let him add. He will have quite enough to do to remember the number he is to save for the next column, let alone

thinking whether it is tens or units. That is of no consequence, anyway. The main thing is to give him plenty of varied practice to make him accurate. Do not permit him to use any devices to save his memory. He must add always from the beginning straight up the columns, as a business man adds. He must never say 3 and 2 are 5 and 6 are 11. But always 3, 5, 11 and so on till he reaches the end of the column. He must never be taught to write down the number he is to save. He will never do it unless some one suggests it. In subtraction he must write nothing but the minuend, subtrahend and answer. He must not check off his figures in the dividend as I have seen children do. *He must use his memory and his attention to keep the numbers.* But he need not be kept so wearily on one thing. Push on. An example in subtraction has nothing difficult about it if the figures of the subtrahend are all smaller than those of the minuend. Then addition and subtraction may be taught simultaneously. If the upper number is the smaller in subtracting, and the child says '*he can't do it*' and turns to you to see what can be done,— again, I say, do not bother him with explanations. He can take one from the next figure and that makes 13 or 15, as the case may be. Now subtract, and he goes on. Then he must be careful to remember when he comes to the next figure that he took one away and that it is not '*what it seems.*' Do not mystify him, and after helping him a few times he will need only practice and care.

Multiplication is easy, too. Here he has to be careful as to the number he is to save for the next column. But don't stop here. Go right on. Short division will offer no great difficulty. It needs only care.

All the usual ways of teaching children notation and numeration seems to me a waste of time and a "clackering counsel by words without knowledge." If you take it for granted that the child can write the numbers, he will write them. And when he hesitates in reading, JUST TELL HIM. Don't make him think that he has forgotten something which he ought to know. Read, and let him read after you. In a short time he will catch the trick.

You can no more think for your pupil than you can digest food for him.

BRIEF HINTS.

PROF. GEORGE D. SHULTZ gives the following: Make your school a subject of study. Think of it as a thing that can be moulded, beautified, magnified; as something that reflects you; as something that can have your spirit put in it. Think of it as a garden. Look to see that all things in it grow beautiful.

Give variety to your work. Do not pursue a dull round. Be original. Keep the pupils expecting something. Do not let them feel that they have got to the bottom of your attainments at any time.

Be careful about the language you use. Look out for such things as the verbs sit, sat, lay, lie, etc. Use choice language and teach your pupils to do the same.

Become skillful at the black-board. If you can not write easily and handsomely on the black-board, *"stay in" and "practice"* until you can. If you can not draw neatly, a few minutes practice each day in rudimentary drawing will be a great benefit to you. If you are teaching small children and can draw neat pictures on the board it will prove a great stimulus to your pupils.

THE ELEMENTS OF A GOOD TEACHER

is an article by JOHN W. DICKINSON, of Mass. He says: First, the teacher should have a good physical body. The body holds the most important relation to the mind. It is the instrument that the mind uses in performing its mental acts. If the body is perfectly constituted it forms a good medium through which the mind can bring itself in contact with the external world. If it is healthy and strong, the mind can endure hard labor, and hard labor usually brings success. It is not necessary for one to be a genius, that he may make his mark in the world. Well-directed, persistent labor is more reliable than genius. Or rather, the ability to work until a thing is done, (without much reference to opposition) is genius itself.

Good health is necessary to that cheerfulness of temper so necessary to a sound judgement. A teacher who is weak in physical strength may do his work well, but he will do it in spite of his weakness, never on account of it.

Second, a good teacher is generally a good scholar. As a general rule no one can teach more than he knows. The possession of a general knowledge contributes to the power of teaching particular knowledge. A teacher of limited resources is more likely to magnify forms to the neglect of substance. No one but a philosopher knows how to be simple. A primary teacher must be familiar with all that is taught in the schools above his own, or he can not tell what his own work includes. For this reason it is necessary to have thoroughly educated teachers in the primary schools.

It is necessary that all teachers should be masters of the topics they teach, and of as much related knowledge as possible. And this is not all. The successful teacher must know more than the *branches* of *learning* he teaches. The *right training of children* is the end he is employed to attain. This result cannot be attained unless he is master of the true method of teaching. A true method of teaching is the product of a successful study of the human mind.

From such a study it will be found that the learner at school gains real knowledge, only when the teacher presents to him the real objects of thought; that his mind unfolds itself in strength and beauty only when it exercises its faculties in an independent and vigorous activity, and that his moral nature is cultivated only by imitating a healthful obedience to right moral precepts.

QUESTIONING.

The following points are from the pen of PROF. WILLIAM M. GRIFFIN of Newark, New Jersey:

A teacher should not call upon a pupil to recite before asking a question. The rest of the class will lose interest, thinking the question is for the pupil named; when if the question is asked first, all will give attention, not knowing who will be called to answer it. A teacher should not write any copy for a pupil in a hasty and careless manner. But should remember that both a copy and an example are being set.

All questions asked of a class should require them to think. If no thought is required there is no development, and the pupils become restless and disorderly. No teaching has been done in such cases.

The science of phonetics should be well understood by a teacher before attempting to teach reading. Pronunciation cannot be taught by a teacher who cannot pronounce well. If pupils do not know how to adjust the organs of speech to produce a certain sound, the teacher should be able to tell them just how to place the organs. Not one in ten who says *wich* for *which* knows that wh is sounded hw. Never send a pupil to the blackboard to read a sentence with a pointer in his hand. For he will then point at each word and not read naturally, but as follows: I—see—the—boy. He—has—a—new—cap.

No question should be asked of a class in a general way to be answered in concert, if it can be answered more than one way. For if there is such a question put, answers from all parts of the room will come in wildest confusion, as "Yes, mam, "No, mam," etc. Better first say "How many think so?" Or, "Hands up if you think so, and so."

No improper pronunciation or grammatical error in recitations should pass uncorrected. This is a part of the teacher's work. An excuse of *'not time enough* is no excuse. Is it teaching to permit children in recitations to say *'wat'* for *what,* *'wich'* for *'which,'* and such uncouth expressions as *'aint'* and *'haint?'*

A teacher should not call upon bright pupils to do all the reciting on the plea of 'not time enough to hear the dull ones.' The diamond will always be in the rough unless it is polished. The dull pupils will not progress if the pupils who are better favored with gab do all the talking. Bright pupils are as a rule attentive while dull ones are not. Then, let the bright ones listen some. A teacher should not become tired of correcting the faults of pupils, or of telling them how or what to do. Children have rights, and so long as they do not understand a subject they have a right to ask and receive explanations. A teacher should not do for a pupil what a pupil can do for himself, with reasonable effort.

Every lesson assigned should be prepared by the teacher as well as by the pupils. Then will the teacher know how much to expect of a pupil. But one pupil should be permitted to ask or answer a question at the same time. It is not possible to distinguish the correct answer from the incorrect when several are talking at once. It divides the attention of the teacher and the class. Then it is not good manners for one to interrupt another.

One pupil should be permitted to finish his answer before another is called. If the pupil is slow, it discourages him and deprives him of a rightful privilege to tell him that he is too slow and that he may sit down. A second question should not be asked until the first one is disposed of, satisfactorily.

Time should not be given to asking questions not worth answering. Pupils should be required to have permission before asking any question, leaving seat, to show work on slate, or anything of the kind.

There should be a time for everything and everything in its time; otherwise there will be constant interruptions and confusion. And if pupils are permitted to ask and answer questions in a haphazard manner they are inclined to become saucy. Too large a division should not be reciting at once. Twenty is enough. More can be accomplished in fifteen minutes with twenty, than in forty minutes with fifty.

PUBLIC SENTIMENT.

The following from the *American Teacher* is pointed: No teacher should try to be a radical reformer unless he is *very young*. And he should not forget that he is hired to *serve* the people, not to *reform* them. If he must turn things upside down he should resign and take to lecturing. Public sentiment can be elevated by long-continued, quiet, effective work—not by loud talk or flashy measures.

CHILDREN KNOW SOMETHING.

An unknown writer says: We must not underestimate the knowledge of the child. There are some things, and they are not a few, that the bright child knows before he comes under the teacher's care. And for us to dwell with the air of gravity upon such matters, dilutes all our intellectual influence.

We once saw a man devote a half-hour to teaching a class to *"whittle,"* when the majority of them felt that with as good a knife and as good wood they could give the man several points. In the same way we have seen teachers dwell upon teaching a lake, brook, river, mountain, or hill, when some of the class knew more about such things than the teachers themselves.

While we must always make sure that the class is knowing to the facts, it is better to assume their wisdom and aid their ignorance about every-day matters than to treat them as dunces.

ON SPELLING.

From preface to *Gage's Practical Speller:* Teachers should always articulate clearly, and pronounce correctly when giving words for spelling. Never overstrain the enunciation of a word in order to indicate its spelling. Allow only one trial in spelling, either orally or in writing. Spelling can be taught by means of composition. In all the written work which comes before a teacher, words spelled incorrectly should be so marked as to call the attention of the pupil to them. He should be required to make out a list of them and master them.

SCHOOL BOARDS.

From some unknown writer. Remember that school-books officially represent the people. Assume that in fact they conform to the will of the people. Do not assume prerogatives which do not belong to you. Recognize that school boards have rights which you are bound to respect. Never try to indorse opinions in which you are not seconded by the board. Have a distinct understanding with the board as to what they will endorse. So long as you remain in their employ, perform the duties they require of you. Receive their directions as from those who have the right to command. Show yourself willing and able to do what they want done. If you really know how to direct the affairs of the school better than they do, they will recognize the fact if you give them time enough.

INTERRUPTIONS.

To prevent unnecessary interruptions: Have a time for questions. Allow questions to be asked only after permission has been given. Require every movement to be quiet. Those who wish to whisper should get permission.

A minute or two between recitations should be taken to answer questions. Pupils should be required to raise a hand when they wish to speak. During recitation do not permit a question to be asked for any purpose whatever, except to leave the room, by pupils not reciting. Some given sign should be understood for leaving the room.

BEGINNING A NEW SCHOOL.

The first mistake, says the *Schoolmaster*, that is made is to turn the classes back to the beginning of the book for a review. The last thing your predecessor did was to review the work done last term. Common courtesy requires you to consider that he was reasonably honest and painstaking in his work,—thet he taught something.

Your plain duty is to begin where he left off. If you find that the pupils have forgotten a subject, you can review that particular subject in one or two lessons and then proceed in the advance work. You must not consider that the former teacher did nothing. This is a false conclusion. He did reasonably fair work. You ought to consider that though he may have been weak in some points, you are also. No one is strong in all things pertaining to the teacher's calling.

Then do not spend time in complaining of the former teacher's incompetence. Strive to do something yourself.

He is absent and cannot defend himself nor explain his plans and intentions. If he left no record, ask the pupils for the last lesson they recited. Assign the next. Ask no further questions at that time. One or two recitations will show the weak points. Work at those. Do not waste time on what is already known. Do not think of drill or practice unless you have some definite purpose in view. Be sure you accomplish what you undertake.

If the history class are through the American Revolution, pray do not lead them back to Columbus and John Smith. Boys and girls who have studied history much know about Pocahontas. If you read it again, what good? Suppose you find out that some pupil in the class thinks the battle of Brandywine was fought in Massachusetts. You need not review the whole history on that account. In teaching history and following the movement of armies teach the *geography* of the country over which they passed, as well as the events.

If the pupils know the fundamental operations of arithmetic do not go over compound numbers again because one girl in the class has forgotten how many cubic inches in a bushel.

Expect pupils, in reading, to know the subject matter of the text well enough to write down the points of importance if called upon to do so. Do not assign one paragraph, — all humbug,—assign a whole subject and then if it takes more than one lesson to finish it, well and good.

Be sure to teach writing in every way; you can not have too much of it. Let pupils write their recitations quite often, and give them some attention. See that capitalization, punctuation, indentation, and *margination* all get their share of attention. Eternal vigilance, here, is the price of a nicely prepared paper. Expect each paper to be an improvement and make your pupils feel this. Permit no slovenly work with pen and ink. A pen and ink education is what young people need most. Never accept a paper written with a lead pencil after pupils are old enough to write with pens.

Do your best, always. Work other hours beside the time you are in the school-room if you wish to succeed.

Master every subject you have to teach if you must burn midnight oil to do it. Each lesson should be thoroughly imbibed and assimilated by you before you stand before your class to hear it recited.

Also find time to read something of more merit than what you are teaching,—wholly in advance of it. If you intend to be a teacher, get upon a higher plane.

ON RECITATIONS.

An editorial in *American Teacher* says : Study the effect of your assignment of lessons; methods of conducting class-work, manner of addressing children, also their interest in their work, and·never be content until confident that you have exhausted your resources for so modulating your methods as to secure the best tone of work in the school. You are not merely to teach them, but you are to secure for them by your manner and method a teachable disposition. You are to adapt *them* to the lessons, as well as the *lessons* to them.

The fault is more likely to be in the teacher than in the class when there is any general failure. The lesson assigned may have been indefinite, the quantity of work allotted, injudicious, as to the pressure brought to bear upon them from other quarters, the introduction of the exercise unguarded and irritating, the tone of the teacher discouraging, the questions of a dissipating character, etc., etc. Children are susceptible to things to which a teacher is hardened. The teacher oftentimes needs to seek for error within self. Not charge failure to the class, altogether. It would be a fine thing to have some teachers *marked on the scale of ten as to success in conducting recitations and other school work.* Possibly the record made would make them more charitable toward their pupils.

THE TEACHER'S CONDUCT.

MISS BANCROFT says: Never come before your school with a cross or vexed look on your face. Always, if possible, have a pleasant word for your school at the opening of each session. As far as possible, believe in the goodness of each individual scholar. Never punish a pupil with an air of satisfaction. Try to administer reproof pleadingly. Or, if obliged to use severity, do so as though the circumstances of the offense and the welfare of the school demand it, and not your own wishes and inclinations.

Always conduct yourself toward each pupil as though you expect him to obey the rules of the school, and if possible have faith that he will. Never allow yourself to say disagreeable things of your school, to anyone, except to gain some advice.

GENERAL HINTS.

S. P. ROBBINS, LL. D., of Montreal, Canada, says to teachers: You must yourself be accurate. The distinction between the well-educated and the improperly educated is just here,—that the one is, and the other is not automatically and minutely correct in recollection, in mode of thought, in manner of expression. Do not teach anything that must be subsequently unlearned.

With little children, especially at the outset, much attention must be given to them individually. This, however, in many instances, can be done so as to interest others not directly addressed, who may be asked to give the information that their companion requires. Try the following device occasionally: Let the whole class stand. Then as each one answers a question he may sit. This continues until all are seated. Or to facilitate the work in reviews, this plan: Say "all who can answer this question, stand." Then ask the question. And if you have some doubts as to the ability of one to answer it, ask him. Pupils will not be apt to rise unless they are certain of their knowledge of the question. Or you may reverse it occasionally by saying "Those who know whether such and such a thing is so and so may sit." Then of course those who have doubts will feel obliged to rise for fear of being called upon to answer the question.

Holding up the hand to indicate the wish to reply to a question is open to great abuse. Forward children attempt to answer everything, but timid ones, nothing. It is a good rule that the hand shall not be held up except when another pupil has made a mistake. Or when the teacher gives a very hard question and asks the class to indicate their knowledge by raising hands.

Rising from the seat, running after the teacher, thrust-the hand almost into the teacher's face, snapping the fingers, etc., are very improper acts. At times the teacher stands or sits so as not to see the whole class, hence is the cause of such rudeness.

It is impossible to carry on the work with the active co-operation of the teacher in two classes at once. Having given one class an exercise in writing in some way— on slates or paper,—the work having been properly explained, then the teacher should give individual attention to another class.

In examination of slate work with small children, it is better that they bring slates to the teacher instead of her going to them. They can be taught to rise and march by her, depositing slates as they pass and marching on around to their seats without interfering with each other or taking up much time or making much noise. Teacher can examine slates while they do something else. Preparatory classes are not expected to do school work at home. Hence all their books should be left in the care of the teacher.

WITH REGARD TO THE PUPIL.

The following appeared in the New England *Journal of Education* as a translation from Diesterwig:

Teach naturally. Regulate your teaching by natural grades in the development of the growing individual. Begin teaching at the standpoint of the pupils. Guide them from there, onward, steadily and thoroughly, without interruption. Do not teach what is in itself nothing to the pupil when he has learned it, nor what will be useful to him at some future time. Teach intuitively. Proceed from the near to the remote. From the simple to the complex. From the easy to the difficult. From the known to the unknown. Follow, in teaching, the elementary method. Also follow the psychological aim, or that and the practical at the same time. Rouse the pupil through the same topic presented from as many points as possible. Combine, especially, knowledge with ability, and exercise the knowledge until it is shaped by the underlying train of thought. Teach nothing but what the pupil can comprehend. Do not simply train and polish. Education and discipline are not for this, but to lay the general foundation on which to build the character of the individual, the citizen, and the nation. Accustom the pupil to work. Make it for him not only a pleasure, but a second nature. Recognize the individuality of your pupil.

With regard to the subject taught,—apportion the matter of each subject from the standpoint of the pupil, and, as indicated already, according to his development. Divide and arrange the subject matter so that, where it is practical in each succeeding step of the new, the relation of what has been taught may be seen. Connect all subjects which are especially related. Go from the *thing* to the *sign*—not the reverse.

Be guided in your selection of a method by the nature of the subject. Arrange the subject taught, not according to a special scheme, but consider, constantly, all sides of it.

With regard to outside circumstances of time, place, order, etc. Follow up subjects with your pupil successively, rather than together. Consider the probable future position in the life of your pupil. Teach with reference to a general culture.

With regard to the teacher: Strive to make your teaching attractive and interesting. Teach with energy. Make the subject to be learned, palatable to the pupil. And above all, require a good utterance, sharp accent, clear statement, and thoughtful arrangement. Do not stand still. Rejoice in development or progress; first, for yourself; second, for your pupils.

RULES FOR TEACHERS.

Author unknown. Teachers should give personal attention to the order of their pupils in passing in and out of the school-rooms, and should watch carefully over their conduct during recesses; should see that boisterous noises, throwing, boxing, wrestling, scuffling, etc., are not permitted in the school room or halls; should use due diligence in securing the attendance of all pupils in the district entitled to school privileges; should not inflict bodily punishment upon any child above the age of fourteen years, without first consulting the parents or guardians; and in all cases of difficulty between teacher and pupil, the

teacher should be presumed in the right. Teachers should
have watchful care over the morals of their pupils and
their conduct. Also their hygienic habits,—as to the state
of health *every day*, and *cause* of *ill-health.*

THE NEW EDUCATION.

PROF. AARON GROVE, of Denver, Colorado, says to
teachers : Do not accept and appropriate the many devices,
short cuts, and patent methods, recommended to you
through the professional press, just because some well-
advertised name appears as the deviser. You read about
a new education, an unfortunate misnomer. There is no
new education. A new combination of methods, different
groupings of appliances, re-arranging of causes and
sequences, are the study and practice of the profession.
No more newness pertains to the work this year, or last
year, than has appeared every year for the past quarter of
a century.

If you are working in your school-room with all the
originality, personality, and genius that your studies and
your ambition can awaken, yours is a new education quite
as much as the great something, which is sometimes now
written as a proper noun.

By study, observation, experience, contact, conflict,
and consulation one with another, teachers learn to *make*
and not to *appropriate* methods. The Chinese exactness in
imitation is fatal to excellent teaching. The science must
precede the art, and in a certain way the art must be
original.

A tendency appears amongst a peculiar school of teachers of pedadogies,—and the number is temporarily increasing,—to preach the ease, happiness, heavenly bliss, and
contentment of the pupils in all school relations. They
announce that the beautiful work of the kindergarten can

and should be continued through all grades of school life.
Their sermons tell of perfect schools, where all is perpetual joy, where tears and regrets do never enter, where
tasks cease to be tasks, where geography is mastered by
playing with mud pies, and the science of numbers appro-
priated with "confectionery plums." When punishment
is uncalled for, all is continual bliss. They print pretty
statements, or permit others to do so, which appeal to
popular prejudice and parental devotion. They talk of
wrongs perpetrated upon the average pupil, and of the
unreasonableness of demanding results. What wonder if,
when a father sees his boy on the high road,—as he is
told,—to eminent scholarship, and that *journey made without pain, discipline,* or *anxiety,*—made because the boy loves
to apply himself,—what wonder if the fond parent is
enthusiastic about that school.

My friends, your experience has already taught you
that he who performs an assigned task usually does it upon compulsion; not from love of work. In child life, as
in adult life, some drudgery is necessary. Do not be discouraged at these declarations about loveliness : they are not
true. The multiplication table must be learned, somewhat
by force memory, however Grube may assist. Elementary
knowledge never was and never will be coaxed or wheedled
out of or into the average American school boy. Sterner
discipline is necessary.

Pleasant and happy schools are the only good ones.
But all this rot about leading a pupil through the eight
years of our elementary training, with only continual pleasure to him, deserves the condemnation it will receive, while
its authors will soon disappear from the school platform.

THE NEW EDUCATION, AGAIN.

The following extract from the *Illinois School Journal,*
of Oct. 1887, upon the subject "New Education," has some

bearing upon the teacher. The editors in their comments are finally led to say: We hold that some things are self-evident: 1. *The teacher must know the child, physically, mentally, and morally,* and the laws of his growth along these three lines. 2. *He must know the subjects that are to be taught to the child* in a larger and fuller sense than they are now generally known. 'The great need of the schools is scholarly teachers. 3. *He must know how to use this knowledge of the child and of the subjects, so as to stimulate the largest and best growth in intelligence.* It is along the three lines here indicated that education must grow, and the necessities of the present age have given marked emphasis to the first and third of these requirements.

We have little confidence in any educational leader who ignores any one of these, or who is so blinded by the light of one method of procedure that he can see no other. *We deny that there are short cuts,* or *essentially new methods* and processes of educating children.   .   .   .   .
As to method, we deny that "American pedagogy means the art of wheedling children into learning things without their knowing it," as our English critics affirm. But we are compelled to admit that if much that passes current as *"new education"* is to prevail this definition will hold.

The teacher must be a fountain of patience and kindness, and love; but a fountain of vigor and intelligence, also.

CHAPTER VI.

DISCIPLINE.

In 1884, J. S. BABCOCK, of New York city, published a manual of the Board of Education of that city. Some extracts from it are here presented: "True objects of Discipline."—The training of pupils so that they *form right habits and learn self-culture* is the true object of discipline. In all rules and methods of discipline employed, this purpose should be kept steadily in view. Discipline, in its relations to order, exists for the sake of the pupils and the school. It prepares the way for the work of instruction, and makes it effective. *Obedience* is the first condition in discipline. It includes conformity to requirements as to time, place and manner, such as punctuality, regularity, orderly habits, etc.

Like begets like. Then "as is the teacher so will be the school." It is therefore requisite that teachers should possess fixed habits of neatness, cleanliness, and order; gentleness of manner, a watchful self-control, and a cheerful spirit. In speaking, let pleasant tones of voice prevail. Then the words of reproof will be more impressive and effectual.

Teachers should never forget that their pupils are constantly and closely watching their conduct, and are prone to imitate whatever they observe. Pupils should, therefore, see and hear nothing that they may not safely imitate. There is an "unconscious tuition,"—the silent influence of which produces the most permanent effects.

Encouragement inspires confidence. Children, more than others, need encouragement. It is a strong incentive to effort. Let it be given in all cases where it can be wisely done. In class discipline, especially, is this needed in cases of timid pupils whose reserve causes them to speak with such a low and hesitating voice as not to be understood. A proper degree of encouragement will render them confident and spirited, eager to tell what they know, and in an audible tone of voice. Letting a boy know that you believe there is good in him is the best way of putting it there, and promoting mental improvement as well.

A development of public opinion among pupils in favor of right and against wrong, will give the teacher a lever with which to handle individual members of the class. Give proper attention to those cases of disorder in single pupils, — a disorder that cannot be overcome through influence upon the class. *Success in discipline does not lie in telling individual pupils their faults before the class.* Neither will right public opinion be developed, nor pupils be led to a willing compliance with the wishes of the teacher, by attempting to detect and correct each individual misdeed. Judicious commendation, when pupils make efforts to overcome faults, is more effective toward accomplishing the desired results, than any system of suspicious espionage.

No system of education is complete if it neglects to provide for physical training. Children should be taught how to sit, to stand, to move, to walk; to abstain from the use of things, and to avoid the performance of acts which are injurious to the health. Cleanliness of person, and of clothing; the importance of breathing pure air, of eating proper food, of caring properly for the eyes, the ears, the teeth; and the necessity for daily physical exercise should receive special attention, and be made subjects of instruction and admonition. All the regulations and instructions regarding these things should be simple, and should be incidentally brought in, and with discretion.

ABOUT FRETTING AND TALKING.

E. M. HARRIMAN says: I wish, as teachers, we might realize how little is accomplished in the school room by fretting. Such an indulgence must bring every teacher, thus guilty, to a realizing sense of loss of power, and it inevitably weakens the teacher's hold upon the child. . . . I have been surprised to see how little talking on discipline is really necessary. There is another advantage in silence, which, though secondary, is of value. A boy who is disposed to be unruly, never knows just what policy you intend to pursue in case of an offense, and he is less likely to venture.

In most instances, lectures delivered to a class as a whole, produce a profound and even distressing effect upon the *very pupils for whom the remarks were not intended.* So, that the conscientious pupil who is straining every nerve to meet all the requirements, and keeps up with his work, is rendered nervous and unhappy, while the *real offenders* depart in peace, because they have not been obliged, personally, to face the subject. Usually, their school consciences are not sufficiently sensitive to be much affected by anything but a personal application of the truth.

Then why waste time and strength in doing what not only does no good, but actually produces just the results which all kind-hearted teachers most deplore? The answer must be, the impatience of human nature. It is better to wait and call the offender to account, privately. The advantage in this method is, that you have a surer opportunity to rouse the better feelings of the offender, and one thing sure, you do not arouse some of the worst emotions, as is certain to be the result if you call a boy's name publicly and humiliate him before his schoolmates. A boy once told me, that all the boys generally stopped work, in cases of public reprimand, to see who would get the best of it, the teacher or the pupil; that is, whether the scholar was conquered and humbled, or only roused to bitterness, though he dared not reply. Of course exceptional cases may arise where it is necessary to disgrace a pupil publicly, but such instances are very rare and require excellent judgment. Speaking hastily may work off the teacher's ill feelings, but it works them *into the scholars' dispositions.*

CAST-IRON RULES.

SOLOMON SIAS says: More teachers fail in securing good discipline in the school-room through lack of discrimination than through most other causes. It is for this reason that cast-iron rules are so detrimental. They allow no discrimination in their application. Children have a very delicate sense of what is right, and many a teacher has fallen into disrepute with them through his failure to discriminate between an accidental and an intentional violation of law, right, or propriety.

I knew one teacher who, in his ambition to have good order, would punish for all violations without distinguishing between the accidental and the intentional,—and each with similar severity. The children learned to hate him. The fault was not so much in his rules as in his administration of them. So is it with many others.

We must look carefully at the person, the manner, and the apparent intention. A look, a slight motion, a kind word is all that is usually needed when there is a violation of some conventional propriety, some school regulation, or when some accidental disorder occurs during school exercises. A pupil who evidently intends to misbehave, requires summary and it may be severe punishment, both for his own good and for that of the school, but the average teacher punishes ninety-nine who are really innocent, as well as the one really guilty.

SOME FURTHER HINTS ON DISCIPLINE.

AMANDA J. YOUNG is the author of the following:

Discipline, when taken in a broad sense, includes all the appliances of school life. In a contracted sense it refers to the correction of errors and faults. If the order is bad in school the fault is with the teacher. The teacher fails, first, to command respect. Second, to note, and promptly correct the little faults of her pupils. Third, to demand the strictest obedience in the smallest thing. For example, if a boy is seen wearing out his jaws, or their hinges, on a piece of rubber chewing gum, and you request him to put it in the stove, and instead, he thrusts it into the coal-bucket or out of a window, send him for it, have him to throw it into the stove, *and nowhere else.* You thus teach him that nothing short of exact obedience will answer. The teacher must have an ideal school in order to entertain a hope of reaching the real. Every effort must be like that of the painter, or artist, to let every stroke of the brush make the *fancied* picture a *real* one.

To attain good discipline it is not necessary to abuse the many for the faults of the few. Neither is it necessary to take scolding-spells three to five times a day. Nor to deliver a lecture an hour in length, thereby wasting the time of the pupils besides cheating the patrons.

Some teachers, like some house-keepers, allow things to take their own course, and then have a general straightening day. But the keen eye of the ever-watchful pupil, like that of the mariner, sees the gale at a distance, and hurries to make ready the ship. He knows, also, that when the storm ceases, an undisturbed calm will follow, and he can again unfurl his sails.

Some teachers feign not to see many things that occur in school; either from indifference, or to shield some *favored pupil.* Again, many teachers persist in saying every half-hour, "Order, here! Less noise!" They are surprised that they have *more* noise and *less* order, and are often obliged to give up the attempt in disgust.

Silence is the basis of thought. It is the soil in which it grows. Its purpose is therefore two-fold; to give moral strength, and thought power. It need not be death-like. It need not be the ghostly stillness of a church yard. *But it must be respectful and uniform.* At intervals there may be the rustle of turning leaves or an audible hum of voice; but it must be the hum of busy industry instead of idleness and mischief.

Punctuality is a great leverage in securing good discipline in schools. Let the teacher set the example, and be prompt in everything. Let everything be done in season, and at a stated time. Such conduct on the part of the teacher will inspire to systematic habits on the part of the pupils.

ON SUSPENSION.

The *Chicago Inter-Ocean* said, but recently: A very large majority of the pupils of the public schools can be governed by *moral suasion.* The parents know it; the teachers fully recognize it, and would scarcely consent to teach if it were not so. As a rule, also, the best teachers have the fewest cases of corporal punishment, often managing their school for weeks without an instance of it. Yet these same teachers attribute their success in part to the fact that they have always had the power to maintain their authority by physical means, if intellectual and moral arguments failed.   Undoubtedly the easiest thing for a teacher to do with an unruly pupil is to suspend him. Then, for a month, if no longer, he is rid of all trouble from him.   This effectually sets him back into the next grade, because he gets behind all his classes, and it probably so discourages him that he stays out of school altogether.   Of course the school is purified.   After a time none but those who scarcely need a teacher to instruct them in good behaviour, remain, and all is lovely.   *The well need not a physician.*   The physician in this case being a *paid salary*, is not concerned about the loss of his patient.

LIBERAL DISCIPLINE.

Miss Wadleigh, who was for several years connected with New York Normal College, said: We do not aim at the martinet in discipline, to lay down rules for physical movements and attitudes.   What we wish are *simple, unaffected, lady-like* manners, which adorn alike the class-room, or the drawing-room.   The merry laugh at intervals of recitation, is always a welcome sound.   Herbert Spencer asks "if sportive activities allowed to boys do not prevent them from growing up gentlemen, why should a like sportive activity allowed to girls, prevent them from growing up ladies?"   To a certain extent we indulge this merry activity, and I think we see in the cheerful faces that surround us, how much better a liberal discipline is than that which is constrained and stereotyped.   There should be no correction or discipline, whether thé offense be light or grave, which does not enforce some moral lesson.

RESTRAINT AND FREEDOM.

An unknown writer says: Order limits attention to the work in hand.   In reality the amount and kind of work attracts the attention, and is the essential means of keeping order. Two questions may be confidently asked: "Is there too much restraint for good work?" "Is there too much freedom to command the best attention?" The only thing to be done is to make the work, the greatest of all surrounding attractions.

It is simply cruel to try to prevent a child's talking a little about his work to his neighbor. The frantic attempts to stop whispering would be ludicrous if they were not so unmerciful.

Self-control is a growth that too much restraint stultifies. Precision is necessary for accurate and orderly arrangement, but when precision steps over the line and encroaches upon the freedom necessary for thought evolution, it cripples and deforms.

No one can mistake the happy, joyous atmosphere of a good school-room. I am quite sure that I can feel the growth of a school, and the best place in which to judge of it is the play-ground. If the children break out of the house with yells and cries like prisoners breaking away from the Bastile; if they are coarse and rough in their manners; if insolent to their equals and impertinent to their superiors, then be sure that such a school furnishes but little better instruction than the street. Some teachers work assiduously from morning till night and appear to have fair success in the school-room and yet they have not one particle of moral power over their pupils. The longer such pupils attend the schools of these teachers, the more ungainly in mind and body they become.

KEEPING IN.

Keeping in, as a means of discipline, is thus commented upon by the *New York School Journal :* The pupil is sometimes required to remain in during recess, or after school, as a punishment. The plan has been sharply criticized.

Many never employ it. Very many steadily use it. It is no uncommon thing in some schools to hear at the close of the exercises, " John Jones, Mary Johnson, etc., may stay in." The rest of the pupils file out, but these pupils sit still; nor do they seem to feel very bad about it. In fact, they chuckle to themselves, " The teachei has to stay in, too." Upon careful inquiry, we shall find that about the same pupils " are kept in " every time.

Is this a good plan? Certainly the teacher ought not to be kept in. It works a wrong to him. Why should the pupils be kept? The causes are numerous—whispering, tardiness, poor lessons, sauciness, disobedience, etc., etc. In fact, if there is anything wrong, the pupil is told to " stay in after school."

As to staying in during recess, we pronounce that bad, unless the teacher send the pupil out before recess or afterward. To wholly deprive him of recess is a wrong to his physical needs.

As to staying in after school, we say that the teacher should aim to abolish it root and branch. It should be permitted to those pupils who desire advice, information or assistance.

But some will say, " What am I to do for all these other offenses? " We ask you if keeping in prevents tardiness, whispering, etc? A long experience leads the writer to doubt the efficacy of keeping in for any offense. Usually the same pupils are kept every night.

Years ago the rod was plied vigorously for tardiness, sauciness, etc. Teachers then thought it indispensable. They quoted Solomon to sustain them if there were any doubt. But the rod has been laid on the shelf and " keeping in " is the cure.

In a large department myself and two splendid assistants daily had from ten to twenty delinquents to attend to.

There were lessons to make up, tardiness, disorder, etc., etc. In settling these up, an hour was usually consumed. At the close of one these sessions, one of my assistants declared that he believed we created in the pupils a habit of staying in. It startled me. I investigated. There was John W——, who, a month before, had never been on the list of those who were to " stay in." Now he was on the list steadily. I determined on reform. The next morning I told the pupils that I wished to go home when the school was out that day, and would thank them to have every thing right. To oblige me they behaved handsomely, and I marched home when they went. By a steady effort the habit was abolished. . . . .
There are better plans. Rolls of honor, reports sent home, and the good opinion of the school are far more effectual.

As soon as possible, the teacher must lift his school up and up, until it is on the basis of an assemblage of friends in his parlors at home. But some teacher will say, " That could never apply to my school." . . This is not all fancy. Rough boys treated as though they were worthy of good treatment *will respond.*

A plan must be made to cover the sauciness, disorder, etc. And here the teacher's skill in management will be apparent. For lack of a good plan for his campaign many a general has been beaten. The teacher must study his school and determine that for want of mere skill in management he will not " keep his pupils in " the foul air of a school-room longer than is needful. Besides, he needs the fresh air himself.

LOVE AND DISCIPLINE.

PROF. RAAB says : Children can be happy only when they feel that their teacher loves them. They have a very fine sense for detecting the love of their teacher. They ask

for love, for they were all made to be loved.   But it is not
necessary for the teacher to tell them continually of his
love for them.   When his love is genuine, the pupils know
it without words.   In school where love dwells, the teacher
may be strict, *Oh, so strict,* and · the children love him
nevertheless.   But in order to be successful, love must be
coupled with justice,—love must be consistent.   This becomes evident, especially in the matter of punishment.
He only ought to be permitted to administer punishment
who punishes lovingly,—who punishes to reform.   The
rod is most effective in the hands of the teacher who loves
his pupils.   Love and true happiness can be found in
school only when the teacher loves his profession,—when
he is filled with holy enthusiasm for his cause.

The first requisite of the public school is vigorous discipline, and strict moral education in truthfulness right-
eousness, honesty, and conscientiousness in duty, decency
and reverence.   These virtues must not be neglected.
Children must be guided in such a way that labor is joy to
them.

THE BRIGHT, MISCHIEVOUS BOY.

LILLIAN M. MUNGER, of Wellesley, Mass., says: It is a
simple thing to acquire and keep order in school.   A task,
not easy, perhaps, but whose difficulty is greatly lessened
by a little forethought and management.   Have you not
noticed that the mischievous pupil is often the bright, active boy who never fails in his lessons, and who receives
the punishment for his misused activity in a manly fashion.
His shortcomings only demonstrate the truth of the
familiar sentiment, that a certain unmentionable person
always finds "*mischief for idle hands to do.*"   ·

If the author of the trouble received the punishment,
the consequence would not be so disastrous; but since the

chastisement inevitably falls upon the boyish instrument of his folly, the question becomes rather more appalling. It is only in obedience to a natural instinct, we know, that a child is always in motion;—a fact which should not be ignored in the discipline of a school room.

It is not possible that the physical development of the organs of a school boy may be hastened prematurely or that he should cease their vigorous use. Only in Sunday School books can such a phenomenal case be known.

Reducing the problem to its simplest mathematical form, it reads: "Given, a bright boy to find how to keep him from pinching Jimmy or sticking pins into Johnnie." *Rule:—Keep him busy.*

There are numerous ways of applying this principle. Have you in your ranks a dull pupil who needs more assistance than you can give? Tell your mischievous boy about it, and ask him to clear the matter up. Use tact, and he will understand that he is conferring a great benefit upon himself as well as increasing his own importance in the estimation of his school fellows. If you approach him in the right manner, he can assist you greatly and will never take advantage of the situation. If you are fortunate enough to have blackboards let him put your work on them for you. Let him correct your spelling papers for you, your language papers, your compositions. Let him work out the problems you propose to ask your class in the recitations. Quite a number of boys might he employed in this way. Make use of the active boy, constantly, and never give him to meditate upon anything only his school work and the work you direct him to do. But you need not let him know why you thus keep him engaged. He will quickly conceive and carry out the most startling projects if you give him time to study them out. Hence employment will keep him out of mischief. . . .

Extra work can be assigned to these lively fellows, but it requires sacrifice on your part.˙ It takes extra time. Yet they must be directed toward the useful.

Supply extra reading matter, if possible, for such boys, —something in which they will take an interest. Anything honorable to beat disorder. You must plan to this end. If you burn midnight oil in mastering the details of management, the results will finally meet your approval.

QUESTIONS ON DISCIPLINE.

The following remarkable chapter of ·"Questions on Discipline" appeared a few years back in the *Pennsylvania Teacher*, I think. It is given *"verbatim."*

What is discipline from the teacher's standpoint? What do other people call discipline? Why do you subject your school to such a code? How do you discipline, or manage, or govern? What is the effect,—present and prospective,—of your methods of discipline upon the character and after-life of your pupil? Will a community composed of your pupils be wiser, happier, better, because of your treatment? Does your idea of the term comprise merely the method of government employed to paralyze unquiet bodies, to silence active tongues, and to touch with apathy all the emotions of the human heart? Does it mean punishment, chastisement, correction? So that you sing with Cowper:

> "Plants raised with tenderness are seldom strong,
> Man's coltish disposition asks the thong;
> And without discipline the favorite child,
> Like a neglected forester runs wild."

Does it not mean the application and enforcement of those principles and rules which regard the purity, order, efficiency, peace, and well-being of your pupils? If a school is designed to develop head, and heart, and hands,

harmoniously, must there not be training of the heart, as
well as the others? Is the discipline that you enforce in
the line of this training? Rather do you not discipline,
mainly, with the thought of your own bodily comfort in
view, that you may have a good, easy time in your teaching labor, that your tongue may have uninterrupted sway,
and your brain free activity, unchecked by the wilfulness
and waywardness of children?

But how do you discipline? Do you speak in the loud,
imperative tones of the taskmaster, driving unwilling
workers to toil,—as one who will not brook denial? Do
you speak with the dictatorial air of one born and bred to
the purple and the scepter? Do you play the part of the
bully, the virago, or the shrew? Do you saw the air with
hands, and gesticulate, and attitudinize before your little
world with all the empirical graces of a cheap actor in a
dime museum? Do you shut your heart, as well as your
eyes when you open your lips in judgment, and refuse
evidence that would be granted to the vilest criminal in a
court of Quarter Sessions? Do you, whenever an act is
done which merits your disapproval, ever seek to find the
inciting cause? Do you ever try to find the cause of the
whispered word? Or the restless movement and laggard
attention? Is there an inner pleasure to your displeasure?
Do you lie in wait and spread a net to snare the feet of the
unwary? When a fault is committed and you,—all justice
—pronounce sentence, do you ever think of the words of
Burns,

> "One point must still be greatly dark—
> The reason why they do it."

Do you ever think of changing places with them, and
subjecting yourself to the same treatment that you are
dealing out so lavishly? Do you ever think that the

"golden rule" applies to them, as well as to you? Do you ever think that the community created the school wholly for them? Or was it created for you? Do you not know that the education of the heart is possibly of more value than the education of the head? That ideas of justice, and mercy, and fair dealing, and regard for the feelings of others, and pity, and charity, are all very valuable adjuncts to modern society; and that possible criminals are made by your methods of disregarding human rights, even if they are wrapped up in child bodies? And above all, and over all, do you ever think, when you are dealing so unmercifully with bodies, ideas, and principles, and grounds of action,—do you ever think of the homes of the children? Do you not know that the home governments, and trainings and surroundings are as diverse as the flowers of the fields? That the ideas of persons, manners and principles in those homes may be entirely at variance with your ideas upon the same subjects? That the child with his home affection believes that his parents are right and that they can do no wrong? What does your pupil know of the home skeletons that are found in almost all houses? What of the hidden vices, ignoble practices, nervous temperaments, and domestic infelicities? What of the poverty, or crime, or ill-health that cast their baleful shadows around, and effect every view, and influence every thought? Do you think that a child who is subjected to such influences, can readily, quickly, and cheerfully come under your sway, without a jar? Do you not know that a perfect, manly, sensible discipline involves the co-operation of four different parties,—the school authorities, the parents, the pupils and the teachers; and that all four must be in complete accord before success can crown their efforts? Have you never felt that as a disciplinarian you are a failure? Have you not experienced the pleasure of receiving the applause of the great republic for work well done? Have you not been esteemed for your successful efforts in moulding the intellect and shaping the destinies of those committed to your charge? Would you "hide a multitude of sins" by converting one sinner from the error of his way, and saving a soul from death?

"HOW CAN WHISPERING BE PREVENTED?" by MARION TALBOT, translated from the German, contains some excellent advice.

Hardly a lesson passes by but the teacher has occasion to complain more or less of whispering, which interrupts the instruction, if it does not render it altogether fruitless. What can be done?

In order to give a satisfactory answer, it is necessary to find out (1) who whispers, (2) what is the reason for it. If whispering is constant and general during school hours the teacher is to blame. If only a few whisper, they are so-called chatter-boxes who can not refrain during the lessons, from sharing their thoughts and observations with their neighbors.

Every class has some scholars who can not keep from chattering, whose tongues are never quiet, who very soon tire of any teaching, and who then yield to their own thoughts and communicate their views to other children. They are thoughtless and playful. Commands and censure are of but momentary service, because they are used too often and are not commensurate with the cause. Each fault should have its peculiar remedy. These noisy ones must be isolated in order to be made harmless. They should be given a separate place, on the end of a bench, or on a seat by the teacher, so that they shall have no opportunity for whispering.

If whispering prevails in the whole class or during certain recitations, the teacher's method is not suitable.   He
goes on too slowly or too quickly, speaks monotonously or
too rapidly, is too wordy or expresses himself in phrases
which the children do not understand.   Then he should
correct his own faults.

In general, whispering is caused by a lack of interest
on the part of children, and by their need of activity and
occupation.   *Idleness is the source of all vices.*   Accordingly
the teacher should know (1) how to awaken interests, (2)
how to occupy the children and make them participate in
the instruction.   .   .   .   .

Then, the entire cure for whispering rests, simply, in
the inquiry, "when and for what reason do the pupils
whisper?"   They are tired, either because they feel no
interest in the lesson, or because they lack employment
and active perticipation in the work.   If these causes are
removed the evil will be reduced, at least, to the minimum.

CHAPTER VII.

THE RECITATION AND HOW TO SECURE ATTENTION.

THE OBJECTS OF A RECITATION.

The objects of a recitation, G. DALLAS LIND says, are:
(1.) To ascertain what the pupils know of the lesson assigned. (2.) That the pupil may exercise instruction from the teacher and other pupils,—upon points not yet discovered by himself. (3.) That he may learn how to study and investigate. (4.) That he may, by the opportunity the instruction affords, learn correct habits of *expresion*, both oral and written. (5.) That any erroneous notion he has concerning the subject, may be corrected.

He might have added, also, a (6th), That the pupil may "catch the inspiration," and be filled with enthusiasm, which will cause him to push on to something higher, nobler,—to attain the mastery of every subject that tends to make him better.

A writer, who calls himself Pedagogue, says of the first of these objects: Questions should, as a rule, be such as will not suggest the answer, and should always, if possible, be in such language that the pupil can not assume in the language of the book. First determine if the pupil has clear ideas upon the subject. If he simply repeat the words of the author, ask him to explain what he means, and by various questions, compel him to state the thought in his own language.

The lecture system ought never to be used in mixed schools. Pupils who do nothing but listen,—not having been called upon to express themselves, or to form some idea either oral or written, will be found to have no *definite idea* of the subject. The conversational system is excellent when not carried too far. The ability of the pupil can be learned in less time by this system than by any other.

Regarding the second object of the recitation. mentioned, Pedagogue says: The teacher ought to answer questions, brought up during a recitation, only when the different members of the class fail in answering them, and then should strive to bring out all the opinions he could from the class before giving his own."

Of the third object of the recitation as here set forth, Pedagogue says: There is an art of study,—an art in studying as well as in anything else. Few pupils know how to use a book so as to obtain from it the useful points without reading it word for word. Every book should have an index. Show pupils how to use the index, then assign topics to be searched out in different text books. This plan will excite and stimulate a love for study. It also enables the pupil to depend upon himself to a certain extent.

RECITATIONS IN YALE COLLEGE.

PRES. ELLIOT, of Hartford, Conn., recently said : The recitation is considered as an opportunity of examining a student to see whether he has learned the lesson of the day, and to give him a mark of merit or demerit has wellnigh disappeared from Yale College. It has become, for the teacher, an opportunity to give conversational instruction by asking questions, addressed either to an individual or to a class, with a view to correct misapprehension and to bring out the main points of the subject clear of the details, by explaining the author in hand, or by contravening, re-enforcing, or illustrating his statements.

For the student it has become an opportunity to ask

questions; to receive either in a critical or in a docile spirit, the explanations and opinions of the instructor; to review the lessons or re-examine the subject of to-day; and to test occasionally his own power of translating, of stating a proposition, a case, an argument, or a demonstration, of narrating a series of events, or of describing a plant, an animal, a disease, a building, a person, or an institution.

If this holds good in college instruction, there are certainly many excellent points in the above for teachers of public schools.

EVERY PUPIL SHOULD RECITE.

GENERAL JOHN EATON said of the recitation : It is the exercise of expression, and, like study, belongs wholly to the scholar. Study and recitation are the principal means of gaining mental power and practical ability. Both are indispensable to the end in view. Recitation has some incidental advantages of its own.

If properly conducted, it induces study. Few lessons . would be learned in any school, if no recitations were required, or if it were known an hour before-hand *that the teacher would occupy the time in lecturing.*

Again, recitation gives distinctness and vividness to acquired knowledge. No lesson is fully learned until it is recited.

It follows, therefore, that every pupil must recite at every recitation or suffer a loss. Classes should not be so large as to destroy individuality. Concert recitation is objectionable. It creates disorder, prevents quiet study, destroys self-reliance, affords a hiding-place for the idle and reckless, and removes the strongest motive for self-application.

All that is practical in education, in every department of life, is developed by recitation. The power of action, no

less than the power of expression, is gained by this, alone.
The child learns to walk and talk by walking and talking.
The mechanic learns to use his tools by *using them.* He
never could have gained the power in any department of
skilled labor, to perform his work, by *hearing lectures.* In
each department *he learns by reciting.* The skilled musi-
cian has gained his wonderful ability to use the voice and
the instrument by years of patient recitation. The states-
man and orator whose eloquence moves the Senate and
attracts the attention of admiring nations, has gained his
power to influence by *the practice of oratory.* And so the
art of easy, graceful, and intelligent conversation and ele-
gant composition is acquired, by conversing and writing.

HOW TO SECURE ATTENTION,

by Dr. Edward Brooks gives some excellent hints.

He says: A teacher must learn to secure the attention
of his pupils, if he is to succeed in his work. There can
be no high success in the art of teaching, without this
ability. When every mind is intent upon what the
teacher is explaining, the pupils understand and remember
the subject presented. When the minds of the pupils are
inattentive and wandering, his instructions will make no
impression upon them; his words will, as it were, pass in
at one ear and out the other. And let it be remembered
that when the teacher fails to secure and hold the attention of his pupils, he fails in his avocation.

If so important then, how is this art to be attained?
With some it may be a natural gift. But it is an element
of success which all may acquire if they will understand
and practice the conditions.

These conditions may be embraced under two general
heads :—a teacher's *manner* and his *method.* That is, he
can secure the attention of his pupils both by his manner
of teaching and his method of teaching.

By his manner, we mean the personal peculiarities of the teacher, as manifested in the act of instruction.

A teacher should have a clear view of his subject. Clearness of conception leads to clearness of presentation. A hesitating and obscure statement of a fact or principle wearies the mind and dissipates the attention.

A teacher should not speak too fast. Rapidity of utterance distracts the attention. The mind unable to fully grasp the subject, loses the relation of facts, and thus becomes confused, and wanders away from what is being presented.

A teacher's voice should be properly modulated. A sweetly-toned voice charms the ear and wins attention. A teacher should speak with natural and artistic modulation. He should not speak too low, for that will require too much of an effort on the part of the listener; nor too loud, for that confuses the mind and distracts attention.

A teacher's position before his class should, as a rule, be a standing one. In this position he manifests more animation and interest in the subject. His attitude and gestures will attract the eye and do much to secure attention. Besides he has better command of his pupils, and can check the tendency to a wandering mind. If a teacher is seated when hearing a recitation, and his pupils are inattentive, he will find, by rising before them, that he will instantly recall their wandering thoughts, and fix their minds upon the subject he is teaching.

A teacher should be interested in his instruction. This is the *sine qua non* of attention. Interest begets interest. The flame of interest in the teacher's mind will kindle a flame of interest in the pupil's mind. Attention can not be compelled. It must be enticed. The warmth and glow of the teacher's heart casts a glow of interest around a subject that makes it attractive to the pupil, and thus secures his attention.

Method next: By the teacher's method of teaching, we mean those forms of instruction which he employs in communicating knowledge, or conducting a recitation.

He should, so far as possible, teach without the textbook. A book in the teacher's hand often seems to build a partition wall between the minds of the teacher and the pupils. A constant reference to the book breaks the spirit of interest that should flow between the minds of teacher and pupil

The teacher should assign topics miscellaneously. If pupils *know* the *order* of the topics or questions, they naturally allow the attention to wander so long as there is no danger of a question coming to them. If they understand that a question may fall anywhere, they keep wide-awake so as to be ready for it when it comes.

A teacher should use the concrete method, as far as possible,—especially with young children. The mind follows the eye; and the attention is caught through the senses. What is seen is much more attractive than what is only heard or thought.

MAKE THE RECITATION CHEERY.

In the *New England Journal of Education*, the following thought occurs: Every recitation should start off brightly. Say nothing until you can say something cheery. It makes the blood chill to hear a teacher introduce a class exercise by reference to the stupidity exhibited at the last recitation.

OBJECTIONABLE PRACTICES IN THE RECITATION.

Again, from the same source, the following: One of the most objectionable practices in recitation is the habit, still tolerated in many schools, of the children thrusting up their hands, beating the air, and snapping the fingers whenever a special question is put to one of their number. The result is, confusion of the mind, and intimidation of the spirit of all save the few whose power of rapid phrasing and ready-reckoning bring them to the front in this cheap sort of competitive recitation. Every pupil in a class has a right to a quiet and respectful attention, and ample time and favorable conditions for putting his knowledge of a subject into suitable language.

The great difficulty of our graded school work is that the brilliant group at the head will do the work, and the rank and file be left practically untaught, and this very habit of which we speak is one of the most mischievous in producing such a result.

Length of recitation : The recitation of a primary class should continue no longer than ten or twenty minutes. Short study and recitation periods, alternating with recreation, will characterize the daily program of the wise teacher. Plenty of hand work and seat work for small children.

The teacher must not talk too much in the recitation. An unknown writer says: To attempt to hear a lesson by doing all the talking ones's self, is like trying to make a web that shall be all warp. How flimsy such a fabric would be! No child has truly learned his lesson until he can tell it. No, not until he *has told* it. There may be a vague impression of it floating in his mind, but it needs to be definitely drawn out and expressed to make it a fixture. Here lies the great difficulty of those who attempt a course of study by themselves. If they have some friend with whom they can talk over the lessons every day, they will double the benefit. Hence the reason for and the value of the recitation. We fix anything in the mind by telling it

to another.   We make it plain to ourselves by the very
effort of explaining to another, whether it is our teacher
or companion.

Another illustration of the paradox that *giving is getting*
and that *imparting is keeping.*

Do not question a class in regular order—so that the
questions can *be picked out.*   Be sure to light down upon
the listless and inattentive one, and wake him up if no
more.   Be sure every one has had a question, or more, in
every lesson or there will likely be complaints.   A good
questioner knows how to make a lesson pass off with enthusiasm, and a wholesome exilaration for both parties,
that leaves no margin for mischief and disorder.

THE ART OF QUESTIONING.

The art of questioning is found in the *New York
School Journal*, as follows: Much bungling work is done in
the school room by those who do not question in a natural
way.   Having no definit idea of what is to be accomplished
by questions they fire them off in a haphazard way.

By means of proper questions, the pupils are led to
comprehend and analyze truths, are shown their own errors
in reasoning or apprehension, and their minds are roused
to attention and activity.   The teacher is able, by skillful
questions, to determine the mental habits of individual
pupils, to rebuke the indifferent, to check the too assured,
to encourage the despondent, and to improve the language
of the pupils.

There are two kinds of questions—those that require
simple facts in answer, and those which require answers
in regard to the relations which facts bear to each other.
The former may be styled *what* questions and the latter
why questions.   The question should depend upon the
mental development of the pupil.   It should be rather

above than below his attainments, in order to stimulate him to greater exertion. For example, in the geography lesson are two questions: "What is the capital of New York?" and "What was the necessity of digging the Welland Canal?" If you ask the latter question of the dull boy of your class and the former question of the bright boy, the dull boy is discouraged and the bright one disappointed. But by reversing the order of the questions, the dull boy has a chance of showing that he knows something of the subject, and the bright boy has a chance to display his brightness, and both are pleased.

All questions convey more or less information. Let them convey all that the case demands, but no more.

Example: · John is called to recite in history. You wish to know how well he has prepared his lesson. If you ask: "John, in what year did the Dutch settle New York?" you tell him three facts and require him to tell you but one. On the other hand, suppose you aim for the question to convey as little information as possible. It contains four facts; a settlement was made, at a certain time, in a certain place, by a certain people. You might ask, "What happened in 1613?" or "What did the Dutch do?" either of which would be bewildering, because too indefinite. The other question would be, "When and by whom was the first settlement made in New York?" Make your questions definite, but not too communicative, and ask questions that will bring out the important facts. Ask them in logical order. Keep the steps of the process clear in your own mind, and by your questions lead the pupil to take them in their natural order. Thus, you are training him to logical thinking. The aid given by the teacher is only temporary, while the investigation to be carried on by the pupil should be permanent. The teacher

should seek, therefore, as fast as possible, to give him the
power to ask his own questions and to pursue his investi-
gations unaided.

Again, from an editorial in a recent issue of the *New
York School Journal*:   There is a way of making the young
listen, with ears, eyes, mind, and soul.   What is it?
Interest first.   This secures attention which can not be
commanded or scolded into action.   Natural tones of voice
must be used.   A pleasant manner is essential.   Good
elocution is requisite.   Don't harp on the same string.
Above all, get responses.   Draw out your audience.
Encourage your listeners to speak out in meeting on all
proper occasions and express their minds. . A little contro-
versy will hurt nothing if properly controlled.   A narra-
tion of experiences is excellent.   Tell stories and draw
lessons from them.   If a funny story, all the better, if the
fun is not low in character.   *Never contradict.*   It is death
to attention.   If you have any very important personal
lesson to enforce, on a very unattractive subject, imitate
Socrates.   He commenced a long way from his application
and asked a simple question that was sure to bring an
answer,—the answer he wanted,—and then another, and
another, until his listener, in spite of himself, was compelled to admit the truth of his argument.   .   .
.   .   The most cultivated minds can not give attention to one subject for any great length of time.   .
.   .   .   It is very difficult for some people to give
attention at all.   .   .   .   .
Intense attention produces absent-mindedness.   It is
said that Sir Isaac Newton desired that his servant should
carry a hot stove out of the room to relieve him of the
oppressive heat.   And that a wag stole his dinner before

his eyes and he afterwards thought he had eaten it because he noticed the empty dishes.

Benjamin Franklin punched the fire down in his pipe with the fingers of the young lady who was sitting by his side.

Pupils sometimes look as though they were giving attention when they are not.

What does all this prove? Only that the teacher during a recitation or at any time he may demand the attention of a class must possess the power of the keenest discernment—*must know* whether he has the attention of all his class. And he must know how to vary his exercise and prevent that stupor from stealing over it,—a thing sure to follow, if attention flags.

CHAPTER VIII.

TEACHER AND PARENT.—PARENTS VISITING SCHOOLS.—TEACHERS VISITING PARENTS.

PARENTAL VISITATION.

But a few years back, the *New England Journal of Education* presented its readers with an editorial upon the subject "Parental Visitation: Its Uses and Abuses."

Some leading points will be here presented: Our valued contemporary, the *Boston Traveller*, deplores the fact that parents do not visit schools more generally, and compares the primary and grammar schools of our city to large orphan asylums, in which parentless children are taught at the expense of the State.

If the editor of the *Traveller* is writing against space it is all very well; but if he really intends to start a boom of parental visitation in the schools, it is hoped he will not succeed.

It sounds very plausible and proper to say that parents should visit the schools to show their interest, to establish sympathy with the teachers, of which sympathy the dear little children are the connecting links, etc., etc. But the fact is, that parental visitation of schools on a considerable scale is a very serious annoyance. This sentimental talk about bonds of sympathy is about a quarter of a century out of date. People are not fools. They know what is going in the schools, altogether too well: They know it by their children's manners, their language, their progress, and that, too, without anybody being guilty, intentionally or unintentionally, of telling tales out of school.

The hours of school are too short to have any considerable portion of them occupied with *"parental chatting with the teacher"* as the *Traveller* suggests. The children are doing well enough, and the teachers are doing well enough. And if the public have confidence in the system, the way in which it is administered, and the *personnel* of the corps, it is just as well to let well enough alone.

The *Traveller* suggests that children never do so well as when in the presence of their parents. True, the presence of the parent in the school-room is a temporary stimulus; but, like all other stimulants, it is unhealthy.

Again, imagine all the parents present, or any considerable portion of them, for any considerable portion of the session of a school! The presence of parents in the school-room is usually a source of embarrassment, to teachers, pupils, and parents themselves. In a majority of cases of parental visitation the parents feel foolish. The teacher is glad when the visit is over, the children are glad, and the parents gladest of all.

Most of this visiting is perfunctory—and performed by the less judicious parents,—generally the mothers.

It is a bad sign of a woman; it puts the idea into one's head, of calling her Mrs. Jellyby, to see her making aimless tours of the schools. It suggests a disorderly household.

It is a worse sign in a man,—an indication that he is out of business, or that he is a professional philanthropist.

The best plan is to give the schools good teachers, and then let them alone.

If the teachers are not good, the children will soon find it out and let the parents know.

Visiting schools by parents should be done with a purpose, and not an excursion of idle curiosity and impertinent meddling by the latter.

In essaying to govern without corporal punishment, good use can be made of parental visits, by special request of the teacher. The proper stand for the teacher to take is that the school is all right. In case of discipline, with corporal punishment out of the question, before the child is suspended, the parent should be summoned to the school to answer for the conduct of the child, and the parent's responsibility for that conduct. This should not be a pleasure trip for the parents,—but rather a disagreeable duty,—a duty which in most cases proves so irksome to the parents that they generally assume a degree of responsibility for the child's conduct, and an interest in his school deportment that almost invariably results in an improvement which could never be brought about by a capricious, or even judicious use of the rod.

Parental calls may be utilized in avoiding corporal punishments, by inviting the mother to come and have some understanding regarding the nature of the offense. Invite her twice or three times, and if this does not prove efficacious, call in the father as a last resort, before the suspension of the pupil.

In such cases parental permission, or requests that the pupil be punished by the teacher should never be acted upon. The people who most earnestly request you to whip their children are the very ones to make the most noise about it when it is done, especially, if, in the heat of the chastisement and through the resistance of the child, the punishment is carried a trifle too far.

We are not against parental visitation, but only suggest that it is not wholly an unmixed good, and that the absence of it is not so dreary and deplorable a state of things as one would imagine.

A school may be as busy and happy as a group of ants,

till the advent of a visitor produces an effect of a spill of water, or the dropping of a pebble.

"VISIT THE PUPILS"

says Miss M. V. GILLIN, of Newark, New Jersey. She says: I have found nothing which has helped me so much in discipline as visiting the parents of the children in my class. It has proved beneficial to go and see the good pupils, as well as the refractory ones. I have known boys and girls who would work hard for weeks for the sake of a promised call from their teacher.

I remember what induced me to try this plan. One afternoon I made a friendly call upon a lady with whom I am acquainted; her little girl was in my class at school. The next morning, in childish fashion, this child tried to make an impression upon her young friends, because the teacher had called to see her. She was proud of the fact and did not fail to show it. This caused a jealous feeling among her playmates, and several of them stayed after school to invite me to their homes. Among them was a girl who had given me considerable trouble by her love of fun and corresponding dislike to work. "Why, Emily," I said, "do you wish me to call upon your mother and give the report which I must if she asks me?" Emily's face showed that she had not thought of any report being asked or given. Finally, I told her that I would wait about a month; if I knew then, that I could tell her mother she was doing well, I would gladly call. From that day there was a change in the girl; she steadily improved. At the end of a month, or a little later, I called upon her mother, and was able to tell of very satisfactory work.

After that I found this was as good a reward as I could give. There seemed to be an understanding between my pupils and myself, that I would call occasionally and give

a good report if they deserved it.   Of course it took time
to accomplish this.   Often I have enjoyed the visit; and I
feel sure that I have gained a number of life-long friends
among the parents whom I have met.

I have also been compelled to call and give accounts
which were anything but pleasant for the parents or myself.   But it has always proved beneficial.   I never regretted a visit.   I have always made it a rule to take the good
reports to the mother and the reverse to the father.   The
mother never fails to repeat the good account to the
father;—yes, and to nearly everyone she knows.   In nine-
teen cases out of twenty the mother believes her child, and
even if she does not she will shield him from the father.

In a long experience of teaching, I have learned that,
usually, where the boy is most annoying in school, the
father is too severe with him, and the mother too lenient.
Very few boys go unspoiled through such training.

Sometimes I have managed a case of this kind by writing a letter to the father.   Instead of sending it, I would
show it to the boy and give him another chance.   Often I
have kept the letter for months without having any further
trouble.   Then, again, I have had to send it, or see the
boy's father.   I would never go to a man and tell him
his boy was the worst in the class, even if I thought he
was.   I would try and find at least one good quality.
While I rehearsed his faults, I would tell, also, the good
side of that boy's character.   No man believes *his* boy to
be the worst one in school; and, after all, there are *very
few totally depraved.*   .   .   .   .   Children go
home, sometimes, and tell all they can of what they have
seen and heard at school.   At times, the truth seems
entirely lost.   Not that they mean to be untruthful, but
very few people can repeat a story exactly as it is; even

grown people fail in this respect. Children, in telling things, use language that no teacher would think of using. I know this to be a fact. People often think their children imposed upon, when, if they knew the truth, the teacher would have their entire sympathy. But parents have no time to call and do not even write to investigate. The teacher seems to think it is not her place to go and see them, and so the matter is left.

There once arose a misunderstanding between one of my girl-pupils and myself. Her mother came around to settle it. I confess that I dreaded meeting her. I had heard of some things that she had said, and so, knew that she had come to settle *me* instead of the difficulty. I never saw a more complete change in anyone than I noticed in her after I had talked with her a few minutes. I quietly stated the facts and found that she had heard a very different story. She took my part at once, and the girl has been my firmest friend ever since.

Another instance,—a boy, who had always been studious, suddenly grew lazy and neglectful of his work. I tried in several ways to arouse his interest, but failed. Finally, as he began to be impudent, I wrote a note to his father. The father's reply convinced me that the boy was encouraged at home against his teacher for some imaginary cause. Instead of writing again, I saw the father. I never had trouble with that boy again.

I have sometimes found it necessary to call several times, in case of a very troublesome pupil. The father, with his manifold duties, often forgets that he has promised to keep an eye upon the work of the boy at school. I would not advise calling to an extent that would make it wearisome to the teacher; but take the time to go to the father instead of detaining the boy after school. You will

be out in the fresh air the sooner by this plan. I have
sometimes surprised a boy who expected to remain, by
dismissing him as soon as the class had gone. Then he
would receive a second surprise when his father came
home at night, if I had succeeded in meeting that father
in the meantime.

A teacher who is fond of studying character, will have
plenty of opportunities by following this course.

Often, the interviews furnished a great deal of amuse-
ment. For instance, the German will promise to "lcek
him," and the Irishman to give him "a good batin."
Either party is equally astonished when I assure him that
I do not want the boy whipped. They seem to think that is
first, second, and last thought of the teacher. Then they
will sometimes ask in a hopeless sort of way, "What shall
I do with him?" My reply is, usually, about this: "Insist
that he do his work."

I have called to see some of my pupils who were rich,
and in many cases have been touched by the way in which
I have been received. One shy little boy in my class was
ill, at one time, with diptheria. I wrote to his mother,
saying that I was sorry of his illness, and that I hoped it
would not prove serious. As soon as I dared, I called.
His mother told me that he was so pleased because I sent
the note, that he asked her several times the next day after
she received it, to read it to him; and each time he would
say when she had finished, "My teacher does care because
I am sick, doesn't she, mamma?"

Among the poorer classes, especially, a visit to the
sick child is considered a great favor. During my short
calls, in this manner, I have learned that "the teacher"
occupies a place in their esteem far beyond what we
imagine.

HOME INFLUENCE.

This chapter shall be closed with a few extracts from an editorial in the *New York School Journal* of April 30th, 1887.

The author has added a few hints, at different points in the quotations.

"Follow a child from a certain class in society, through the various scenes and duties of a single day, and judge what sort of moral education he is receiving *outside* of the school-room. His ears are first greeted in the morning as follows: 'Get up!' 'You good for nothing, lazy thing, haven't I called you a dozen times?' If this human being happens to be a small boy, soap is smeared in his eyes, or his skin is left half wet, or he is rasped with a hard towel, his hair is roughly combed, and he is sent to his breakfast with a sense of discomfort, that is a good preparation for irritableness during the whole day."

Dear teacher, have you pupils to which this seems to apply? Is there something in their general appearance which suggests to you this very treatment? Some little boys and girls have never in their lives been called out of bed in the morning by a gentle voice. Never have received the necessary morning's ministrations from a gentle and loving hand. Know nothing of that kindness, so sunny and winning, so soothing and impressively instructive, so effectual as to good results, which flows from the hearts, souls, lips and hands of many Christian parents, and which should pervade every home of little boys and girls. Then, if some little waifs, unacquainted with anything which tends to make home attractive, fall into your hands, your mission is kindness, forbearance, pity, tenderness, love, sympathy. You need to do something more than drive into their blunded little brains the abstractions of text-books. If they know not kindness at home, Oh, be kind to them yourself! Be not uncertain as to who they are, either. Single them out and endeavor to pour a little sunshine into their souls. You can find them in every school. Their countenances are a sure index to the kind of homes they left in the morning. You have only to study this index from day to day to see the hearth-stone at night, or the breakfast-room in the morning.

Again, says the *Journal* : " At the table he is permitted to remonstrate passionately, with hasty answers and sharp, quick blows in return. ' Oh, I don't like this.' ' Give me some better, I say.' ' Ma, Jim's kicking me.' Thus he swallows his breakfast. With no loving good-bye from mother or sister, he rushes out into the street or road in a proper mood to knock down the first boy he meets upon the slightest provocation."

" Probably, just as he is leaving, he hears the shrill voice of his mother, calling, ' Here, come back and do your work. This is the way you sneak off, is it?' The boy answers, ' Oh, *must* I do the work. I haven't time. Let Jim do it. He hasn't done a thing this morning,' etc., etc. So he goes on."

Now, again, dear teacher, do you wonder that some boys are hard to control? Can you get any hold upon his nature, his mind, his feelings? Psychological, theoretical, practical pedagogy comes in right here. It is for you to apply it properly.

But to go on with the *Journal:* ''Now in what condition is this boy for school work? Half-washed, unfitting clothes, uncut hair, dirty finger-nails,—altogether in about as uncomfortable a condition as a boy can be, especially if it rains. No doubt he fights his battles and encounters his difficulties all along the way to school. There, he may not be greeted with pleasant faces; he finds his teacher cross, work begins with a command, and he is scolded for not having done his *home tasks.* . . . . He doesn't like school, never has, and probably never will."

Again, dear teacher, if this be a true picture, can you wonder at his indifference to school? Are you that teacher? Are you guilty of making the school-room more unpleasant to such a boy than the home described?

But let us follow this boy a little further. The *Journal* says: "When he reaches home he hears the command 'Go and do your chores'; or 'Hurry up and do your work, you can't have supper till you do.' Thus scolded, accused, half-clothed, half-fed, out of sympathy with his surroundings, is it any wonder that he early learns to find his pleasure among boon companions like himself, where the parents are called the 'old man' and 'old woman,' and where such amusements as are known to average young men are popular? What else can he become? Parents of such children are not consistent Christians, however much they profess. There is no uplifting power to instill early, high ideals of good living. The influences are downward, and, under like circumstances, must always be so. Our criminals come from this class, and in spite of all that can be done they must for many years continue to be the breeding places of crime and ruin."

Then, all the more, should the teacher seek to establish closer bonds of sympathy between himself and the parent, as well as between himself and pupil. *The relations already exist.* Strengthen them by learning more of each other. Visit the parents and get them to visit the school.

CHAPTER IX.

EXAMINATIONS.

MANY POINTED REMARKS.

COLONEL FRANCIS W. PARKER said, recently, of examinations in the public schools:

The great question for the superintendent or principal of any school to decide is: Has the teacher the ability to instruct children in the proper manner and by the best methods?

It is possible for a principal to find out in one hour by a series of set questions, more about the standing of the pupils of a certain department, than the teacher who watches carefully the development of these same pupils for one or two years?

Those who understand children will readily appreciate the excitement and strain under which they labor when their fate depends upon the correct answering of ten disconnected questions. Some of the best pupils usually do the poorest work in the confusion that attends such highly wrought nervous states.

How much better, then, is it to take the entire work of the pupil for the whole year than the results of one hour under such adverse conditions. Is the common standard of examinations a test of real teaching?

The examinations usually given simply test the pupil's power of memorizing disconnected facts. Take for example, the innumerable facts in history. Of these, that which a child can learn in four or five years of vigorous study would be as a drop of water to the ocean. It would be a simple matter to set an examination of ten seemingly easy questions in history for eminent historians like Bancroft, Curtius, Dreysen and others to pass and yet *they* would fail, utterly. How, then, can we judge of a child's knowledge by asking ten questions?

The only just way to examine pupils is to find out what the teacher has taught, and her manner and method of teaching. Examinations should find out what a child *does* know and not what he does *not* know. . . .

The *test* of such work, then, (history) is to request the pupils to tell orally, or on paper all they know about Columbus, Walter Raleigh, Bunker Hill or other interesting subjects they have studied.

It is very easy for an expert to judge,—in examinations,—of the true teaching power of the teacher in such work, by the written papers. If meaningless words have been memorized, if there is a lack of research, investigation and original thought, the results will be painfully apparent. Whatever the teacher has done or failed to do, can be readily comprehended by a Superintendent who examines the development of thought power, rather than the learning of mere words. In the same way Geography and the Sciences may be examined. The test of spelling, penmanship, composition, punctuation, and the power to use correct language, can be made in no better way than by the writing of such compositions as these. .

. . . By far a greater part of all school work consists in a useless pilgrimage through a barren desert of empty words—a fruitless Sahara. The cause of this is not far to seek. The examinations demand more than the children can perform. What teacher ever received a class from a lower grade fully prepared for the work fixed by the examination for her grade? Suppose children have

been in school three or four years under poor teaching
and know not anything thoroughly,—can not read, write,
reckon, or think.   Now the teacher who takes such poorly
prepared pupils must choose one of two courses.   She
must do these children the greatest possible good by teaching them thoroughly what they have failed to learn, and
then fail entirely of passing the uniform examinations, or
by sheer force of verbal memory teach them the pargraphs,
pages, and propositions necessary for the coming test.
"Having," says Spencer, "by our method induced helplessness, we straightway make helplessness the reason for
our method."   .   .   .   .

The teacher who teaches for promotions and examinations can never really teach.   The only true motive must
spring from the truth found in the nature of the child's
mind and the subject taught.

Superintendents should examine to ascertain whether
the principals under their charge have the requisite ability
and knowledge to organize, teach and supervise a large
school.   The examinations of the principals should test
the teaching power of the teachers.   And lastly, the
teachers should test by examinations the mental growth of
their pupils.   This is the true, economical system of
responsibility.

First, ascertain whether superintendent, principal and
teacher, can be trusted, then trust them.   The answer to
this proposition, I have heard a thousand times.   "Your
plan would be good enough if we had good teachers.   The
fault is, sir, the teachers are so poor we can not trust
them.   If we did not examine in this way, they would do
absolutely nothing."   The fallacy of this answer may be
exposed in two ways.   First, a uniform examination of
disconnected questions presents the good teacher from

exercising her art. Second, the poor teacher will never be able to see the wide margin between good work and the work she does until the true test of real teaching is placed before her. There has been legislation enough for poor teachers. Give good teachers a chance. The testimony of countless good teachers has been uniform in this respect when asked, why don't you do better work? Why don't you use the methods learned in Normal schools and educational periodicals and books? "We can't do it. Look at our course of study. In three weeks or months these children will be examined. We have not one moment of time to spend in a real teaching."

No wonder that teaching is a trade and not an art. No wonder there is little or no demand for books upon the science and art of teaching—such as Payne's lectures and the like!

THE SYSTEM IS BAD.

A recent issue of the *New York School Journal* contained the following editorial comment:

Much has been written against examinations that ought to have been said against the methods used in them. Examinations are good. They have always been good ever since Adam began to examine and name the animals as he was commanded.

Technical examinations are good when it becomes necessary for the public good to ascertain how much a certain individual knows. Ministers, doctors and lawyers have always submitted to them on entrance into the professions to which they respectively belong, and if *we had a profession of teaching*, it would be necessary on *entering it* to require a thorough and searching examination.

Technical examinations in our graded schools are necessary. Without them the whole system would fall to the ground. The system is bad, and therefore the examinations are bad. But as tests of promotions, according to constituted authority, they are unavoidable.

A school examination should be, primarily, a test of mental power. The question, "How much does this child know?" is far too low an estimate. It should be, "How much mental power has this scholar?" An examination that tests mind strength is excellent.   .   .   .   .

Pupils should never dread an examination. Fear is evidence of weakness.

There should be no cheating during an examination. It ought to be so conducted that there would be no temptation to cheat. When an examination is so conducted that deception is suggested as a means of getting through with it, there is nothing of value connected with it.

Their frequency, special ways of conducting them, their method, as written or oral, public or private, must be left to the teacher, and the circumstances surrounding him. An examination that tests mental growth and promotes it, is good. One that does not is bad. They should be conducted according to normal laws of human nature.

EXAMINATIONS BY ESSAYS.

WILLARD BROWN said, Education should be a training to promote insight, power of thought, and facility in acquiring knowledge.

Perception, not memory, should be cultivated, and as the student can advance, only by his own endeavors, he should be led through such a course of labor and original thought, that he may come out an independent thinker, as well as a thorough scholar, in such branches of education as he has inclination for.

To obtain such a training, *examinations* should be means, not ends.

For example, instead of the student in political economy, history, philosophy, or mathematics being obliged to
work, as now, with an examination of catch questions,
perhaps,—it would be better to let it consist of original
essays in the first three subjects, and the performance of a
paper of great severity in the last,—all being done at the
student's leisure and with such assistance as he can get
from books.

RANKING BY EXACT PER CENT.

In the *School Journal* (New York) of May 23rd, 1885,
may be found the following editorial comment: School
examinations should be conducted by the teacher.   They
should never be made the basis of a marking or standing.
The pupils during the time should feel that they have the
opportunity of doing their best, because by so doing they
can *improve themselves.*

At the close of a term, grading marks should never be
published.   Those who are to be promoted should be
informed of the fact, and the rest permitted to remain
where they are, or placed in a lower class.

The evil of ranking pupils by exact figures, differing
often by a fraction of one per cent., only, is sure to create
unnecessary pain,—to appeal to low incentives,—and to
awaken feelings that ought to be banished from the school-
room.

No class was ever ranked correctly by a column of
figures.   It is impossible to estimate all the elements of
success in school work by any mathematical exhibit.

It is manifestly improper to leave out many important
elements in solving the problem of the exact precedence
and place of pupils in a class.   Why omit promptness,
cheerfulness, application, honesty, common sense, quick-
ness, helpfulness,—all these, and rely entirely on the stock
questions in the three R's?

No set of examination questions can tell a faithful teacher nearly as much, after it has been given, as she knew before the examination commenced.

Good work, hard work, persistent honest work, *the best work*, can not be encouraged by empirical examinations. An examination, like anything else, may be good, bad, or entirely worthless. Its value depends upon its character.

RESULTS ARE THE TESTS.

GEORGE A. LITTLEFIELD, of Newport, R. I., says: Examinations, wisely conducted, are a process of teaching as well as of testing. They are reviews pure and simple, with the extraordinary power added to compel attention as nothing else can. They must be made the natural outgrowth of the methods of teaching. Results, and not methods alone, must be the test in schools, as in other affairs. Wholesome examinations are the readiest measures of results. Good teachers must be left free to work out the required ends in their own way.

CAN'T DISCARD EXAMINATIONS YET.

The opinion of the author of this little volume is, that *examinations* yet deserve a place in our public school system, for several reasons.

First, whether conducted by a subordinate teacher alone, or partly by the teacher and partly by the principal, if conducted honestly, they reflect that teacher's work as faithfully as a mirror does the expression of the face. There is no better way of pointing out defects in teaching, to a teacher, than to require that teacher to give his classes a searching examination. The teacher, if honest and intelligent (and all should be) will quickly perceive, during the examination, all his weak points, and will do better work during the next interval. Even if, as is claimed, teachers be under the lash somewhat, still, it will do them a great good.

Second, the standing of each pupil is *relatively* established. To be sure, it is by a column of figures. But, they all,—as a class—had an equal chance at the same subject matter. Hence the *figures* can not be far from the proper thing as to relative class standing. And that is one of the objects sought. The decriers of the system say "ten disconnected facts" show no results. This is a false assumption. Ten proper questions in any study judiciously given *will establish this relative standing* beyond question. Still, while the ranks in a class ought not manifest very wide gaps as to different degrees of attainment, say by *figures*, no wider that 70 to 90 per cent., yet, a pupil should not be put in a lower class because his average scholarship is 68 or 69, while another is permitted to remain in his class with an average of,—say 71, or 72. Any sensible person can see that all things being equal, these two pupils rank together. But the line must be drawn somewhere. Stragglers must be cut off, and the ranks closed up. The extremes can not be from 40 to 90 per cent. This is too wide a gap. And figures will show the true state of affairs, as to the class.

Third, as to frequency, there is no necessity of examining at the end of every month as some do. Let the interval be five or six weeks at the discretion of the *chief teacher.*

Fourth, as to objection, that there is undue excitement or mental strain upon children. Again, this is all assumption. Children talk eagerly about the *"examinations,"*—some saying they dread them, and all that. This is natural. Children, like some *"grown-up people,"* enjoy gossip, discussion, and excitement. But they are not seriously harmed thereby. In fact, their wits are sharpened all the more by talking to each other of their examinations. Really they *rather enjoy the whole thing.*

As to the good accomplished on their part:—They learn correct habits as to expression, as to producing neat written forms as business men do, as to concentrating thought upon a given subject, as to exercising the judgment and reasoning powers of the mind, and as to exactness of detail, one of the most essential things in life. Their views are expanded at each successive examination.

Besides, it furnishes occasional variety from the regular routine of school life.

Let those who decry the system, first prove that they, upon the whole, can substitute something better, before we discard examinations in public schools.

CHAPTER X.

SANITATION.

STEAM HEATING.

The following clipping is to the point, but, unfortunately, it is impossible now to give proper credit:

Just now, steam heating of school-rooms is the rage. Pipes extend around two sides of the room. From six to eight children sit with their backs to these pipes, and as many more with one side close to them, while one poor unfortunate in the corner seat has both back and side exposed. There is no screen, and the sickening heat-rays almost cook their tender brains. The air is terribly dry, yet they must breathe it. Headache and faintness follow. Eyes suddenly become hollow, the cheek pale, yet the steam goes on chasing through these pipes. With the room crowded, it is impossible to alternate pupils in these seats rapidly enough to prevent the evil results. Woe to that teacher who dares to express an opinion against this process of brain-cooking, when fashion, the architect and the superintendent have decided in its favor. The only defense is to open the transoms, which allow the hot air to escape and a cold current to rush in, so that all in the room can feel the wind, can shiver, can suffer.

A school-room or any other, is best ventilated by providing for the escape of the impure air *near the ceiling*, and for the entrance of fresh, out-door air not too far from the floor, but in such a manner that persons sitting shall not feel it as wind.

A simple, yet effectual contrivance for turning the draft from the lower part of a window when raised, so as to keep it from falling upon the pupils, is a board so placed as to change the direction of the current.

For some cause, not clearly understood, when depending upon steam heat, if the wind blows, and heat is most needed, it is least sure. And many times a class must be dismissed, or kept shivering through the day, with shawls about the shoulders, but feet and limbs stiff with cold.

HYGIENIC QUESTIONS.

In Canada, the Provincial Board of Health officially issued the following questions, with many others to the teachers of the Ontario schools:

How many cubic feet of air space for each pupil? Is light admitted in front of the pupils, at their left side, or the right, or from behind them? Is light well distributed? How near to the ceiling and to the floor do the windows extend? Have the windows blinds? Is a uniform and equable temperature of from 63° to 70° F. constantly maintained during school hours? Is the air dry? What means are adopted for supplying moisture? Is there any means of testing the temperature? Explain fully how each room is ventilated in all kinds of weather,—whether by windows open at the top or bottom, by ventilating flues, or in what other way. To what expedients do you resort to prevent draughts from open windows striking pupils? Is the air in the room completely changed by opening doors and windows at stated intervals during school hours and at recess? How often is the school-room swept? Do pupils frequently complain of head-ache, cold feet, or any symptoms indicating the existence of defects in ventilation or heating?

What is the duration of school hours and recesses? How are pupils and teachers occupied during recess? At what periods are the greatest numbers absent? Is the water pure, cold and abundant? If from a well, what means have been adopted to prevent its receiving the soakage from surrounding grounds?

Is drinking water kept in the school-house? If so, where is it kept, and how is it protected from dust and other impurities? Are there cellars or other excavations beneath the school-house? Are there water-closets for the different sexes, in different or separate buildings? Are they properly protected from observation and from inclemencies of the weather? State where they are located in relation to school-house, wells, etc. Give distances. What means are adopted to keep them clean? Are they well ventilated?' Is any disinfectant used, and what? If water-closets are used are the traps and appliances efficient? Have you any observations to make respecting the clothing of pupils? Protection against sitting with wet feet, etc? Is there any instruction given in Hygiene?

MEANS OF PROMOTING HEALTH.

At the meeting of the Wisconsin State Teachers' Association, July 24, 1886, Dr. J. H. Kellogg, of Battle Creek, Mich., said: One important means of promoting health is systematic physical exercise. Many kinds of labor and some games furnish the requisite exercise, but most trades lead to some forms of bodily deformities. The teacher should inform himself respecting dietetics, and faithfully instruct his pupils therein. Among the best foods are milk, plainly cooked grains, and fresh fruits. It is a mistake to suppose that large quantities of meats are needed.

Proper clothing and the prevention of the spread of contagious diseases, are topics with which the teacher

should be thoroughly informed, and in which he should give thorough instruction.

DEPRIVING PUPILS OF RECESS.

The author will here take the privilege of adding a thought as a measure of health. No pupil should be denied the privilege of leaving the room during a session of school,—always provided, of course, that the teacher is sure the pupil is not practicing deception. Of course, here is where the trouble lies. All pupils are not strictly honest and much trouble and confusion may arise from pupils passing out. But that is within the scope of discipline and has nothing to do with the privilege. If permission is refused and the pupil is made to remain in his seat when he is not deceiving, then a great physical injury may be wrought upon him. Or the teacher may be humiliated by the refusal. Of course this must be regulated in some way. But it is a right of the pupil, and should not be abolished or abridged too much.

Depriving pupils of recess by way of punishment for some offense, comes under the same category. *The recesses are measures of health.* Comment is unnecessary. If punishment is necessary, resort to some other kind.

CHAPTER XI.

PEDAGOGICAL QUESTIONS.

The chapter of questions here presented may not appear, to the casual observer, as " *ideal*," yet the answer to them may imply an ideal in each instance.

The answer may generally be inferred nearly accurately, and a single question will sometimes open the eyes of a " *truth seeker* " to some defect in his own labors, that may prove a lasting benefit.

ON LITTLE THINGS.

Some one recently writing over the initials E. O. H. in the *New York School Journal*, propounds the following:

Fellow teacher, is your desk in order? Are the books, paper, pens, ink and pencils in order? Is everything in the drawer arranged on a plan? Or is the drawer full of things pitched in? The eyes of children see many things. Are your cuffs and collar clean? If you wear ribbons do they harmonize with the surroundings? Are your finger-nails clean? Is one who is careless in personal appearance fitted to teach habits of neatness? Which should go first, example or precept? Are not the little things of life as important to us as the great things?

QUESTIONS BY A COUNTY SUPERINTENDENT.

The following list was made out a few years ago for the teachers of Marion County, Iowa, by their superintendent, Mr. Sacket:

Have you a carefully arranged program posted up in your school-room? Have you as good order as can be secured under existing circumstances? Are you training your pupils in habits of neatness? Are you doing anything to prevent tardiness and irregularity of attendance? Do you give your pupils frequent and thorough reviews? Do you teach sounds of letters and diacritical marks in connection with reading exercises? Do you permit your pupils to read in drawling, unnatural tones? Do you teach local geography? Are you giving attention to map-drawing in connection with historical and geographical studies?

Are your pupils well supplied with writing materials, and do you give due attention to penmanship? Are the youngest pupils taught to write as well as to read?

Are all of your pupils fully employed during study hours?

Do you keep yourself well informed in regard to current events, and furnish your pupils with important news items?

Do you give close and faithful attention to all school property? Do you keep your school register neatly and correctly, using pen and ink instead of pencil? Do you take any educational paper?

Will you have any questions to ask of the County Superintendent when he visits your township for the purpose of holding a local institute?

Are you personally acquainted with the parents of all your pupils, and do you secure their co-operation in matters of interest to your school?

Do you encourage pupils to think for themselves and talk about the subjects learned from books? Do you have the older pupils write their spelling lessons?

Is more time devoted to any one study in your school than ought to be as related to others?

"QUESTIONS I SHOULD ASK MYSELF" by GEO. H. COOK, of Iowa:

Have I done all I could do, to-day, for the good of my school? Would I do my work again the same as I did, if

I could? Have I used proper language in the presence of my pupils? Did my clothes look as neat as they should as an example for my pupils? Did I prepare my lessons as thoroughly as I should have done? Could I have added any new thoughts to the minds of my pupils on any lesson? Have I read any journal or school-work to aid me in my teaching? Did my pupils speak respectfully of me, and to me? If not, why not? And what reproof did I make? Have I permitted my pupils to be boisterous in the room at recess? Have I asked the patrons to visit my school? Would it encourage the work for them to do so?

Did I call and dismiss all my recitations at the proper time? Have I permitted some point in school discipline to pass unobserved? Has my day's work been fully satis· factory? Did I call and dismiss my school promptly and on time? Have I examined the property of the district to see whether it has been defaced or injured in any way? Have I paid attention to the ventilation of my room? Are there as few classes on my programme as can be? Have I given each class something to do? Do I know that it was done? Have I endeavored to get out of any old ruts to-day? Have I arranged my programme in proper order, and with neatness? Did I fail to make recitations interesting? If so, why?

Was my school so orderly that I was not interrupted during recitations? How many questions did I ask to-day that could be answered by yes or no? Should I have asked any of that kind? If not, why not? Were my general exercises instructive and interesting? Did I proceed with a recitation while there was disorder in the class? Did I have my school-room in condition for opening school? Did my pupils *all* give due attention to the recitations? Have I allowed any pupil in a class to interrupt another? Were my pupils prompt in their recitations? Have I kept a record report of tardiness and absence? ·Have I exchanged ideas with any other teacher? Which topic has been most difficult for me to explain to-day?· Have I assisted any pupil who could have helped himself? If school has gone wrong·to-day, who is to blame? Have I been angry?

ANOTHER GOOD LIST.

It is impossible to give the name of the author of the following list: Do your pupils pass to and from recitations in a quick, prompt, orderly manner? Do they scramble out at recess like a flock of sheep? Do they keep their books and desks in good order? Are there pieces of paper lying around the desks and on the floor? Do the pupils spit upon the floor? Has each one who uses ink a good pen-wiper? Or do they wipe pens on their hair? Do they throw ink upon the floor? Do you insist upon clean hands and tidy appearance, generally? Is there a mat at the door for pupils to wipe their feet upon? If not, can't you get one of some kind? Would they use it if you did? Is there a scraper? Can you get one, if there is none? Do your pupils speak to you respectfully? If one should not, what would you do? Do they call each other names? Are you sure there is no vulgarity or profanity on the playgrounds? If there should be, what would you do? Do your pupils constantly use provincialisms in their conversation without any sign of improvement,—such as "I seen him," "John done that," "Me an her is a goin to town," etc.? How are you trying to overcome such crudities? Do you require them to speak correctly when reciting? Do you permit them to scrawl rude scrawls upon the black-board? Do they mark on the walls with pencils? Do they steal crayons and mark on the

fences as they go home? Do you teach them the proper
way to behave in the streets? Do you allow bullying
on the playground? Do you set them an example of
refined courtesy? Do you think more of manliness than
of book-knowledge?"

. AS TO STUDIES,

from the *New York School Journal :*

Which should be taught first, long or short division?
Why? Which first, common or decimal fractions, and
why? Should we ever teach a rule? If so, when?

Would the study of physiology be worth more to our
pupils than the study of grammar? How often should
school entertainments be given, if at all? With children
thirteen years old should we teach the *how* only, and let
them learn later in life the *why*, or should we teach both
together? What should be done with a pupil who comes
almost every day with imperfect lessons?"

QUESTIONS BY THE AUTHOR.

In written recitations and examinations do you require
your pupils to produce neat manuscripts, as to even mar-
gins, proper headings, correct punctuation, capitalization,
indentation, etc.? Are you content with mere answers to
the questions, regardless of order? Or do you have written
recitations ? If so, how often? Can you teach some other
lesson, incidentally, in the lesson at hand on whatever
subject?

If a pupil produces a written lesson, slovenly in appearance, what can you do? Which do you think more
important, an oral or a written recitation? Do you let
written papers accumulate on your hands without examining them? Did you ever have a history class read from
the book upon a subject, a full recitation one day, talk
upon it next day, and write upon it the third day? Can

you quote Lord Beacon's celebrated sentence upon the above subject?

If your classes are all busy—to a pupil—are you troubled with disorder? Can you distinguish between the noise of work and the noise of disorder? Between intentional wrong and unintentional wrong? Do you ever become so excited during a recitation as to say some indiscreet thing and wound some pupil's feelings? If you should wrong a pupil unintentionally, and afterward learn of it, would you seek that pupil and confess it? How do you preserve your equanimity when assailed by angry and fault-finding patrons? Do you get angry, too? Does that amend the matter? Are you of a sociable turn when not in school, and when thrown in company with the people of the community in which you teach? Or are you glum and cynical? Are you dogmatic? Pedantic?

Do you work as many hours at your private study, to make a success of your school, as the hours of actual school work during the day? Do you burn midnight oil in your plans of a successful campaign? Are you teaching just for a present emergency? Do you attempt any other branch of business, meanwhile? If you do, is it justice to your patrons? Do you get time for professional reading? *Do you make use of the time in that way?* How many educational papers are you taking? How many professional books have you read? Could you name ten leading authors upon the subject of school-teaching? Do you keep on hand plenty of reference books?

Do you study human-nature? Children? Methods? Only books? All?

Do you spend money for professional books and papers and in attending educational gatherings? Grudgingly?

Do you have your classes review often? Do you vary the exercises? Do you keep on doing things the same old way? Have you an *ideal* in your work? Are you working just as willingly and as energetically as you would if your salary were twice what it now is?

Are you a success at organizing classes? At gaining and holding attention? At gaining and holding the respect of your pupils? If not, have you tried to ascertain the cause? Do you give unnecessary directions? Make unnecessary explanations? Talk when pupils are not giving attention? Give orders and immediately countermand them?

Do you permit useless discussions, criticisms and questions? Indolent habits of work? Slovenly prepared written work?

Do you take up time explaining what pupils already know? Explaining what they should find out for themselves? Repeating questions? Repeating answers? Picking at a certain pupil till the rest of the class lose interest and become disgusted?

Do you make muddy explanations to conceal ignorance? Do you expect to accomplish a week's work in one day? Do you forget that you were once a child?

Do you magnify small offenses? Scold and threaten and get excited? Threaten a punishment which you can not inflict?

Do you assume powers that do not belong to you? Assume to be infallible? Do you build up your own reputation by pulling down others?

CHAPTER XII.

MISCELLANY.

THE TEACHER'S OFFICE.

WM. F. Fox, of Virginia, says:

Let us give some attention, fellow teachers, in the midst of our other duties, to the enlargement and elevation of our own conceptions of the teacher's office; to making our fellow citizens more thoroughly acquainted with the teacher's work, and the qualifications needed for the successful discharge of its duties; to the establishment of a more definite, professional standard; to manifesting in our own characters illustration of those quantities that make up the true teacher; to securing a well-defined scheme of education that shall combine all the elements of a thorough education with the shortest period necessary for its successful accomplishment.

DO YOU DO ALL THE TALKING?

From the *New England Journal of Education* the following:

If you are a poor teacher you will do most of the talking yourself; if a good teacher you will have the pupils to do most of it. And if you are a good teacher you will not scold a pupil for stumbling and tumbling before he has learned to talk, nor demolish the bashful boy or girl with a stern " sit down," because he is neither a dictionary nor a grammar unto himself. The good teacher takes his pupils as they are, not as he would have them *a priori;* that is, as he thinks they ought to be, and builds from the foundation as he finds it.

How many teachers fret and fume, and make uncomfortable both the children and themselves, because they find them ignorant where they should be wise, and that their previous training has not obliterated all indications of their descent from old Adam.

EARLY RISERS.

PROF. HUXLEY, on one occasion said: Make haste slowly. The educational abomination of desolation of the present day is the stimulation of young people to work at high pressure by incessant competitive examinations.

Some wise man (who perhaps was not an early riser) has said of early risers in general, that they are conceited all the forenoon and stupid all the afternoon. Now, whether this be true of early risers in the common acceptation of the word or not, I will not pretend to say, but it is too often true of the unhappy children who are forced to rise too early in their classes. They are conceited all the forenoon *of life* and stupid all the afternoon. The vigor and freshness which should have been stored up for the purpose of the hard struggle for existence in practical life, have been wasted out of them by precocious mental debauchery, by book-gluttony and lesson-imbibing.

SOME THINGS THAT OUR SCHOOLS NEED.

The following thoughts are extracts from a lecture delivered at the Industrial Educational Association, the summer of 1887, by W. N. BARRINGER, superintendent of schools, Newark, N.J.

First. Our schools need a more intelligent and cultivated public sentiment. . . It must come from the educational profession.

Second. And schools need more liberty. I know of nothing that is so powerful a hindrance to good teaching as restriction of liberty. It is impossible to estimate to what extent the teacher's efforts are paralyzed or hindered by restriction. There must be more liberty. Let us throw off the bands of restriction, and let the soul of the teacher feel, "I am free to teach." Freedom only can beget freedom. Let us have liberty all along the line.

Third. We need less uniformity and more unity of purpose. . . "Oh!" some say, "but this will lead to confusion." One of my teachers came to me and wanted to know what I thought constituted a fair recitation. I told him to use his judgment. "But how can there be any uniformity of judgment unless there is some standard?" he replied. "Never mind the uniformity," I said. "It is not necessary that to be an acceptable answer, just so many words must be put together in a certain order. Measure the child according to what he can do.

Next. Our schools need more life and less organization. . . I have no fault to find with organizing, if, only, life is left,—if the whole school is not reduced to a mere machine. Too often this is the case, and then it takes all the teacher's time to look after the machine. It takes all the pupils to oil it and keep it going. The teacher is there to see that the marching is done right, that the going in is done right, and the sitting, and the standing, and the turning in the seat, and the looking at the nail-head in the wall ! ! !

MAKE THE SAME MISTAKE BUT ONCE.

In the *New England Journal of Education*, November 4, 1886, is a quotation from the *Educational Weekly*, as follows :

The best teachers are not those who never make mistakes, but those who never make the same mistake twice. Many things can be learned only by experience. No one can understand all the peculiarities of the human mind.

Some new phase of character is seen every day. It is natural to err under such circumstances, but we should each day rise above our faults. No one need ever hope to attain perfection. He must be strong indeed, who never repeats a mistake. Each day weak places in our methods must be strengthened.

LETTING THINGS SLIDE ALONG

MRS. EVA D. KELLOGG says: Looking at the best and ignoring the worst in our children is an easy way of getting through a school year. It is the very high road to popularity. Parents enjoy the pleasant reports from the school-room. Children glide along easily in the smoothly-flowing current. Principals are delighted with teachers who can manage their own rooms without calling upon them.

But can a thoughtful teacher, a conscientious one, who remembers that she is building up character in her children, and who realizes how easily human souls are marred, be willing to thus shirk responsibility for temporary ease? All wise teachers know that there is an injudicious " *stirring-up* " of the worst qualities of the child that is to be avoided as much as possible. We assume that to be understood. Still, we question most seriously the systematic, cowardly refusal of a class of teachers to face issues involving loss and gain in character for fear of consequences.

Can one follow a straight-forward course, a conscientious course, in or out of the school-room and not encounter difficulties?

SYSTEM IN SCHOOL-WORK,

by S. B. HOOD, is the title of an article, in which are found some excellent thoughts.

He says: If order is heaven's first law, it should certainly be first on earth. System has been found essential to success on the farm and in the factory, and will be found equally helpful in the school-room. There is no place where it will lighten labor, save time, and facilitate work more. Without system, a school-room presents a complete picture of hurry and worry, and consequent friction with its resulting waste of power. No wonder sensitive teachers wear out and break down in such schools. To have system we must thoroughly plan out our work and then patiently and perseveringly work out our plans. A definite time and place for everything, and everything in its time and place, should be our rule and practice.

We should be at our school-houses punctually every morning in time to see that fires, floors and desks are in proper condition for the comfort of the school, and the favorable commencement of the day's work.

In beginning school in the morning and afternoon, the bell should be rung twice. The first bell as a signal that school is to be called in so many minutes, so that all may be ready. The second, a call to the school-room, to be obeyed by every pupil instantly. In country schools when children remain at dinner, the time between bells should be about five minutes. This gives time enough to close plays, get coats, drinks, and make all necessary preparations for responding to the second bell.

When signals are once established, they should give out no uncertain sound, but mean the same thing to all pupils every time.

If a school is large, time will be saved and order secured by having the pupils form in lines in the yard before coming in, girls in one line and boys in another, or all together at the discretion of the teacher. If hat and cloak hooks are properly arranged, pupils can hang up their wraps and hats as they pass in, each one having a hook numbered. Another way of disposing of wraps is to let them pass to their seats and have monitors to remove them. Monitors can be appointed by the week or during good behavior. Pupils like to serve. They should not be imposed on by making them serve too long, however.

As far as possible pupils should be seated so that members of the same class do not sit at the same desk. In schools where classes pass out to a recitation seat to recite the plan works admirably. In graded schools, also, for it is almost equivalent to single desks in promoting independent study and good order. In many schools, nowa·days, no passing is done during recitations, except when necessary to use black-boards. But where it is necessary to move classes, signals may be used to advantage. First, call attention of the class in some way. Then count, as " one " for them to face the aisle, " two " for them to stand' " three " for them to pass, etc., etc. Dismissing a class can be done in the same way.

Another great care for the teacher at first is the program. It should not only provide for a time to recite each lesson, but for a time to study as well. If this is not done, pupils will pursue their studies in a desultory manner and accomplish little. Regularity is a gain of time. Program should be on the black-board or on a card written or printed and hung up.

Follow it closely, so that no class shall be robbed of its allotted time, or miss a recitation, for it is discouraging to a class to have a lesson pass by without being recited after it has been prepared.

LESSONS ON PATRIOTISM.

PROF. A. R. SABIN says: Patriotism should be taught in our schools. Lessons in the history and political geog·

raphy of our country have done much to inculcate this
love in the past, as the late civïl war abundantly proved.
But more may be done when better methods of teaching
these subjects universally prevail.

Instead of memorizing a skeleton outline of facts in
history, scores of books should be read in our schools, the
reading to be legitimate school-work.

Books of history, of biography, of travels, of explora-
tion and discovery, of tale and romance, of adventure and
incident, of myth and legend, of fiction, poetry and song.
Such a course of reading would be a historical recreation,
would amuse, delight, instruct, widen, deepen, brighten,
develop and discipline our children as no dry-and-dust
outline ever can.

THE DULL PUPIL.

The dull pupil is written up here by an unknown hand:
The teacher's exertions must necessarily be chiefly in be-
half of the dull pupil. The bright one will get alone with
limited assistance. The dull pupil, thus at once the
teacher's care, is worth the most patient treatment. Let
it be borne in mind that constant scolding will make the
best of us callous, and the dull boy is not brightened by
any amount of reproval.

What is the reason that he seems to have no ambition
to compete with other boys in his class? Why do lectures
avail nothing? This is why: Constant failing has de-
stroyed his self-respect, and he regards himself, in a certain sense, as outside the pale of the general school.

With such a one it is best to try to replace his self-
respect by ascertaining what he can do well. Then encourage him in that. Praise him. Make him your friend.
Make him know that you are his friend. If he is good in
any one study, encourage him in it. If he likes to work

at arithmetic, let him solve examples on the board for explanation to his classmates. If he sings well let him lead in singing. If he draws well let the other pupils examine his work. He will be pleased with all this, and it can be managed so adroitly that neither he nor his classmates need know why it is done.

LITTLE THINGS.

A recent number of the *North Carolina Teacher* contained some excellent ideas under this title:

It is a little thing to put a question to a class the second time, but the teacher who does this to a great extent will soon find himself broken down, unnecssarily. It is not necessary to put questions a second time if they are put plainly at first. Attention in the class avoids this trouble. Ask for attention. If necessary, command it.

It is a little thing to permit one class to consume in recitation a small portion of time allotted to another; but if allowed it brings confusion.

It is a little thing to have a boy ask a question while you are busy; but if tolerated in a single instance you may expect the same trouble to arise throughout the school. You can not afford to lose the time, aside from the confusion it entails.

It is a little thing to permit a boy to leave the room soon after the school is called to order; but let one go unless he has been detained and you would better give a new recess.

It is a little thing to let a boy get a drink of water during study hours; but let one drink and the whole school will almost die of thirst before time for dismissal.

It is a little thing to permit a pupil to borrow a pencil, book or slate; but tolerate it once in one pupil and where can you draw the line?

It is a little thing to permit two to study from the same book or assist each other in their lessons. They seem so kind, don't they? Well, you can not tolerate it. Their kindness works mischief to your school.

It is a little thing to allow a boy an excuse for not being prepared in his recitation. Do it once or twice and see what will come of it. You do the boy an injustice to pass a poor recitation unnoticed. It is a step towards unthoroughness.

It is a little thing to pass a boy's example on the black-board, and tell him it is right, except a slight mistake he had made, it may be in bringing down or changing some sign in a problem in algebra. This will spoil any boy. It cultivates in him a habit of carelessness, that grows as he grows, and it may be the ruin of him.

It is a little thing to hurry over the last part of the recitation, just once, because the time is running short. This grants pupils the privilege of slighting just about that much of each lesson. Better be thorough as far as you go, or as far as you can, and retain what is left over for the next lesson.

As no whole can exist without the sum of its parts, so nothing great can be accomplished without taking in the little things.

THE BEGINNING OF THE SCHOOL YEAR.

The opening of school at the beginning of the school year is a subject brought before the readers of the *New York School Journal*, in issue of September 3, 1887. Several eminent educators gave their views. It is hoped that they will not consider it an offense if some of their ideas are here set forth and preserved.

PROF. JARED BARHITE, of Irvington-on-Hudson, N. Y., says: To a large extent, the opening day will be a day of reciprocal study of character, disposition and attainments by teacher and pupil.

The first day as teacher in the presence of the child, can not be well over-estimated, and should be used to the greatest possible advantage. Here the "tide in the affairs" may be securely taken in hand and directed towards a successful end.

To be at ease, perfectly natural and frank with a child from the moment he comes into the teacher's presence, has more power for good than a score of punishments for offences which are the results of indifference, coldness and reserve on the part of the teacher. An intense interest in the children and their work can not be concealed from them, and they feel and know whether the teacher is working for their interest or merely the salary.

Upon opening school, work should be assigned as quickly as possible. If convenient, a programme of work made out the day before should immediately be displayed. It can be modified afterwards to suit the requirements of the school. An hour of delay wherein pupils are permitted to manage affairs in their own way, may be a fatal hour to the success of the school.

A natural desire on the part of the teacher to make a favorable impression upon the pupils, and a corresponding desire upon the part of the pupils to win the favor of the teacher, may tend to indulgeness and acts which are not fraught with good results. The work should begin as it is the purpose to carry it out.

There are usually some pupils who desire to test the teacher, and ascertain what mettle there is in his composition. With such, the teacher should be frank and aid them in their investigation. Usually these will prove the most earnest and successful workers in the class if turned in the right direction.

There is nothing more potent for good than to thoroughly convince a pupil that you know the trials he has to bear; that you are a friend to direct him in a way that shall make these trials seem less, although they can not be removed; and that you are in earnest concerning his success in the efforts he is exerting to prepare himself for the duties of life.

Wm. M. Giffin, A. M., said: Opening day should be as much like the days that are to follow as it is possible to make it. One should not feel that he must make an address if it be a new school. If it be an old school, then a good hearty greeting should be given in as few words as possible.

There should be no excitement or fussiness on the part of either principal or class teacher. Make all changes so quickly and quietly as to cause the children to forget that they are there for the first time in weeks. Have everything in working order by ten o'clock. Do not allow anything on this day that you will not allow on any other day of the term. Begin and close the school on time, and hear every recitation.

Should it be raining when the children come, see at once that the wrappings of the children, as overcoats, overshoes, shawls, etc., are removed immediately. Inattention to this matter may endanger the health of the children. Some of them are not old enough to have good judgment, and if they err it will be your fault, as you ought to know better. If it is a bright, sun-shiny day do not cause pupils to sit with the sun pouring in upon their heads, or if a cold day allow draft of cold air to blow upon them. Either is pernicious.

From the very beginning, see that the room is properly ventilated. A feeling of dislike for school may be caused by a foul room. Do not begin by trying to startle the class into being orderly or attentive. Children soon learn to wait for the " *thunder clap* " if once begun.

Begin and continue with a low, steady, firm tone of voice. It will accomplish the most in the long run. The desk was not made to pound upon, nor the floor to stamp upon. And neither pounding nor stamping is of th3 least use in obtaining order.

Do not be changeable in your discipline. Be every day alike. Steady, uniform, even, regular discipline must be maintained. " Never a tyrant, always a governor," should be your rule. . . . .

Good teachers are always ready in case of an emergency. A little positiveness is all that is required to subdue a class if it becomes disorderly. Select some pupil and make an example of him. The first one you see out of order very far, is the guilty one for you.

Questions should not be put to the class in such a manner as to call forth answers like " No, ma'am," " Yes, ma'am," etc., all over the room. Avoid this trouble by saying, " How many think so, and so?" or, " Hands up, all who can answer this question." Then put the question. Do not call one pupil's name before asking the question. If you do, the other members of the class will lose interest.

C. E. MELENEY, of Patterson, N. J., said in the same issue: The opening day of school is, to many, one of momentous importance. Here comes the youth, who hopes now, after many futile attempts to acquire an education, to begin a course which he had been looking forward to with so much earnestness.

Here comes the little tot scarcely five years old, who has learned at his mother's knee all his little stock of information, and now enters a new world, where everything is different, perhaps, from his former experience.

Many come who have been impatiently waiting for the teacher to come back, and many who are sorry that life is not one continuous vacation.

All this to the thoughtful teacher makes an instant impression, and he realizes that this is, indeed, to all his pupils an important occasion. And how important to the teacher himself, who, possibly, stands for the first time in the presence of those whom he is about to guide, to instruct and to assist on the way to manhood and womanhood.

The teacher, then, should meet his pupils with an acknowledgement of the importance the opening day is to them, and regulate all his dealings with them accordingly.

Do we, as teachers, realize how we should receive these little ones who come for the first time to this new and strange experience? Can we remember our first day in school? Here should be a warm welcome and a cheerful greeting, never to be forgotten. I have seen teachers take in little children and say, simply, "Go to that seat," or, "Sit down here," with no more consideration than a market-man has for chickens, which he assorts and places in different coops.

What a chance there is to make an impression to win the love and confidence of a little child, and to settle once for all the question of attendance at school.

Everything should be made inviting beforehand. The dress of the teacher should be neat and tidy, and the manner, voice and expression kind and attractive as she bids each one welcome. The room should be made cheerful and homelike.

The teacher should arrive first on opening day, that everything may receive due attention before pupils arrive.

Pupils once admitted become an immediate study for the teacher. What are they here for? How are they to acquire what they needs? How can it best be given? What is their condition of mind? Their present condition of body and heart, in fact? What work is best adapted to their development? What methods should be applied in teaching and management? All these are questions that should be uppermost in the teacher's mind. First learn the pupils.

Devotional exercises claim a share of attention. The mind should be well settled upon a plan, already. There is a wonderful power in music. That teacher is fortunate who can conduct singing exercises. If a teacher lacks this power, there are frequently in these modern days several pupils who can lead out and sing something, and will feel proud of the acquirement if asked to display it. A teacher of tact may always turn this to advantage. Encourage them. The names of pupils may be obtained by distributing slips of paper among those who can write and permitting them to write their names, ages and residence. Learn their names as soon as possible. Call them by their names.

In a pleasant conversational way ascertain something of their qualifications, the books they need, etc. Organize your classes. If it is ungraded, great care need be exercised. If graded they can be divided into groups in a short time according to ability. Don't lose sight of the individual in the mass.

Having found what they can do, give them occupation adapted to their ability. If they have books, assign them lessons to study. Not a moment should be wasted. Take the earliest opportunity to impress the school that it is a place for work.

Accept the situation and be guided by all the conditions that exist.

This being a new experience for some children, make it as much like their former surroundings as possible. Do not put them under too much restraint. Give them an opportunity to move their bodies and limbs. Let them stand and sit and exercise gently. By conversation, learn something of their knowledge and in what they are interested. This is to be the starting point for instruction. Take advantage of the methods by which they acquired this knowledge. Learn nature's way.

It is important to teach children orderly ways in everything—rising, standing, walking, sitting, taking books, cleaning slates, taking care of clothing, cleaning shoes at the door, etc. Each one should have a sponge and slate rag. Have water-bottles and monitors to pass and sprinkle slates.

As all this management will depend much upon the character of the school, make a careful study of all the conditions and adjust yourself to them. Remember that the school is for the children, and that everything must conduce to their success and progress. The development of character is the end at which all zealous and conscientious teachers aim.